GETTING MENTORSHIP RIGHT

Bob Alonge & Samuel Ekundayo

© Bob Alonge & Samuel Ekundayo 2022

Dedication

To our gentle Shepherd, who leads and guides us along right paths, bringing honour to his name.

To all the great people out there who love their neighbors by making the sacrifice to serve as good mentors thus causing mankind to multiply, replenish and take dominion in their world.

Acknowledgments

Special thanks to Rev Adeteju Bob Alonge and Dr Blessing Oluwamayowa 'Dudushewa' Ekundayo who faithfully encouraged us and worked hard to provide the opportunity and environment for us to write this book.

Contents

Dedication — iii

Acknowledgments — iv

Introduction — 1

PART 1 — **3**

Chapter 1: Mentor: Origin and Myths — 4

Common myths of mentorship — 7

Chapter 2: The Mentorship Portals — 13

Chapter 3: Respect Determines Influence — 21

Chapter 4: Three Spiritual Destiny Laws — 26

Chapter 5: Maximising A Mentee-Mentor Relationship — 36

Abuse of mentorship — 59

Chapter 6: The Mentorship Process — 64

We Should Always Prove Them First — 75

Chapter 7: Mentorship Levels and Management — 81

Is a mentorship permanent? — 93

How Do We Correct a Wrong Mentoring Relationship? — 96

What is the level of Vulnerability/Intimacy Between a Mentee and a Mentor — 98

How to Improve the Level of Mentorship With Your Mentor — 100

What do you do if your mentor does not believe in a vision you are pursuing? — 101

PART 2 106

Chapter 8: Mentorship Must Be Gotten Right 107

Chapter 9: You Must Be A Person Of Value 111

Chapter 10: Invest In Their Materials 118

Chapter 11: Meet A Dire Need 123

Chapter 12: Give A Gift 130

Chapter 13: Be Visible - Follow Genuinely 135

Chapter 14: Pray For Them Intentionally 138

Chapter 15: Be Committed To Learning 142

Chapter 16: Know How To Ask The Right Questions 148

Chapter 17: Have A Good Attitude 153

Chapter 18: Pray for Favour 158

Introduction

We all experience some comfort on the journey when not travelling alone. The comfort is even more remarkable when our company has been there and done that. We all need someone else to come alongside us to guide us into the destiny we sense deep within. Moses, sensing the magnitude of the challenges ahead, knew this and invited Hobab to come along him on the exodus from Egypt. Hobab knew the way and was accustomed to the wilderness.

Mentorship is about having a helper in our journey in life, love and leadership. To the mentor, it is an attempt to pass down the experience, wisdom and legacy to the next generation. It is indeed a noble endeavour, yet things often go dreadfully wrong. This book hopes to prevent some of these shipwrecks. It is an attempt to bare our hearts, from our unique perspectives, about the pitfalls of mentorship.

My perspective draws from spiritual mentorship, particularly as a minister who has laboured in God's vineyard for three decades. It is, however, relevant across the board. Sam presents his view from his rich experience in business, leadership and life coaching. Together, we believe that this will offer a robust solution to mentorship going wrong.

MENTORSHIP: ORIGIN, NATURE, AND PROCESS

Bishop Bob Alonge

1

Mentor: Origin and Myths

Interestingly, many people wrongly assume that the word mentor appears in scripture. The word mentor does not appear anywhere in the Bible. The concept that the word mentor and mentorship describes is very much embodied in scripture, but it is critical to note that the word mentor is not in scripture.

The word *Mentor* finds its roots in Homer's Odyssey. It's the name of a character in Homer's Odyssey where Alchemus decided to entrust his son, Telemachus, into the hands of his friend, whose name was Mentor. Telemachus was to be the King after his father passed on. Alchemus was to embark on an odyssey, a long journey that would probably take his life, so he turned to the person he trusted the most, and he said; *I was hoping you could look after my son and groom him to become the next me.*

Now, that idea of discipling somebody to become somebody else or something else is what we have now come to understand as mentorship. We must never forget that Mentor played the role of a eunuch. He, Mentor, was not grooming Telemachus to become Mentor. He was grooming Telemachus to become the next king like his father – Alchemus.

Mentor was not necessarily grooming Telemachus to imbibe Mentor's values, but rather to imbibe his father's values and take the role and the position that life had defined for him. So, that's where we get mentorship wrong in today's world. Many people who claim to be mentoring – and claim to be involved in mentoring – are trying to create clones and duplicates of themselves. We shouldn't do that. The word in the scripture that best describes mentorship is the word discipleship. We are called to make disciples. We need to understand that our job is not to disciple them after ourselves, just like it was with Mentor and Telemachus. Our job as mentors is to help them become what God had ordained them to be. We are to disciple them into the image of the person they are betrothed to; the One who gave His life for us, whose we are and whom we serve – The Lord Jesus Christ.

Our job as mentors should help others mature into the fullness of the stature, or the stature of the fullness of Christ, in their chosen fields, callings, and life. That's what proper mentorship is all about. Like Homer's Odyssey, mentorship isn't about a school you go to; it is an exchange of life. Telemachus lived with Mentor and ate with him, and there was ample exposure and interaction between the two of them.

Common myths of mentorship

Myth 1 - Mentorship Cannot Be Found in the Bible

As I stated earlier, the principle of mentorship is in the Bible. Still, the word 'mentorship' itself cannot be found anywhere in the Bible, and for 'hardcore' Beran Christians, that can be a source of arguments. The word 'mentor' bears its root in Greek mythology, and many things embedded in our modern languages, whether it is English, Spanish, or French, all take their roots in Latin, which draws many things from Greek. Languages and culture are often infused together.

We tend to think mentorship is about creating clones of ourselves, so we try to run other people's lives and remote control them. We often tell them, '*Do it this way*' or '*Do it that way*' because that is what we have done and learnt. Therefore, most of us believe that if you are mentoring or being mentored by somebody, it means that your vision must be directly akin to that person's vision or that your callings must be the same. We suppose their experiences must also be the same as what you are going through, but that is not necessarily true.

Wisdom speaks. Wisdom guides. So, in spiritual mentorship, as Christians, we are supposed to build people in the image of God, not in our image. It's okay if we influence people. It's also okay if people pick up one or two traits from us. But, proper mentorship requires that you must be a eunuch.

What does it mean to be a eunuch? Eunuchs are those that were entrusted with the harem of the king. They took elaborate care of the king's wives and women, but they were not enabled, nor permitted, to derive pleasure for themselves with the king's brides in the process. They knew the women profoundly without having them intimately. A eunuch is somebody who has been castrated. A measure of sacrifice, or self-castration, is essential for mentorship to work genuinely.

When you are mentoring, therefore, you are not mentoring unto yourself. You should be mentoring unto the King, and you should groom the person to fulfil the destiny that the King has determined for that person, not what you want or what you think. That is why mentorship is delicate.

The word 'disciple' parallels the meaning of mentorship. Not only is that word in the Bible, but also every one of us is called into discipleship. It is about us being followers of Christ, being moulded into the image of Christ. So, mentorship is an ideal and appropriate word to use because those that God will place over us are supposed to groom us into our unique expression of the image of Christ.

Every one of us must express the unique dimension of Christ that we are called to, and nobody is called to do everything. Everybody is called to do something. It's about what the King has predestined for each of us, and God will bring people into our lives to serve as coaches, but they mustn't be coaches unto themselves. They are to be coaches unto the King. Their job description is to help you become all that the King has predestined for you to become.

Myth 2 - You Can Have Only One Mentor In Your Life

That is not true. I think that is selfish, and it also comes from insecurity. Sometimes, human emotions come into mentorship. Those who mentor us can become possessive and controlling. Sometimes, they want to cut you off from every other influence.

I recognise that mentorship is always for a reason and a season because it is not a lifetime commitment from the word's origins. Your job is to equip the person until they are ready for their purpose and become like the Father.

Yes, you will have people who will mentor you in different dimensions of your life and people God will put in your life at different stages. Some mentors are permanent, and some mentors are temporary. I will shed more light on this later on in the book.

Myth 3 – Mentorship is Fatherhood

Mentorship is not always fatherhood. Mentorship can be brotherhood, mentorship can be friendship, and mentorship can become fatherhood. Fatherhood is a little deeper than mentorship. Mentorship involves somebody who influences you in the direction your life needs to go. Mentorship is about somebody God brings into your life who helps your life unfold in the predetermined order that God desires. It might involve instruction, correction, admonishment, experimentation, observation, etc.

Fatherhood, on the other hand, is more profound. All fathers are meant to be mentors, but not all mentors will be a father to you. The difference between a father and a mentor is that a mentor does not give you his DNA; only a father does. The seed of a father abides in us. There is a place for spiritual fatherhood, and we will get into that later on.

Myth 4 – Thinking 'Mentor' Is an All-embracing Word That Must Mean the Same Thing in Every Instance.

There are levels and dimensions of mentorship, and we will talk about these in this book.

2

The Mentorship Portals

In life, we learn through four gateways, as seen in Philippians 4:9 KJV,

'Those things, which ye have both learned, and received, and heard, and seen in me, do: and the God of peace shall be with you'.

Mentorship should have four portals of learning: **Observation, Explanation, Experience,** and then **Revelation**. When a child is newly born, you notice that he doesn't learn anything by explanation. You would be a fool to start trying to explain things to a baby. The first things we learn in life are by observation. When a child notices that you give him food when he cries, he will keep crying to get food. The child observes every move you make in response to his cry and associates them accordingly for replication. He has learnt by observation.

Most of the things we learn in life, our first exposure to learning, and our most effective in engaging with somebody else are first by observation. And that's also another way in which many people fail in mentorship. They try to mentor people by what they say, not what they are and do. When God brings you into a relationship of proximity and access where you can genuinely observe without restriction and reservation, where you can observe somebody standing and falling, somebody's joys and sorrows, it's a privilege you must celebrate, not take for granted.

One of the most significant mentorship mistakes people make is assuming that their mentors must be perfect. A true mentor is not fashioning you after himself. He should be fashioning you after the perfect One who is Christ. In mentorship, you are given a privilege that you must honour and respect. It is a privilege to see a person in their strengths and weaknesses so that you may learn by observation. You will not only understand what to do, but also discover what not to do. You would realise that by the person's failures, the person's mistakes, and the person's weaknesses. Celebrate the opportunity to learn what you must not repeat. It is still a part of mentorship and is vital.

So, in mentorship, we learn first by observation, then graduate to learning by explanation. Mentorship is not just putting somebody alongside you, and the person watches you live life; you must also begin to teach, explain, and share. An explanation is also necessary. There are some things that observation alone will never enable you to learn.

For instance, I love how Dr Samuel Ekundayo asks me questions. He will often ask, '*Daddy, how is this, how is that?*' And I speak in return. He inspires me to share, teach, and even ponder, which is what mentorship truly is. The mentee should, through questioning, challenge the mentor to seek solutions that will be beneficial and applicable to his/her life. Therefore, the mentor opens up to share different things the mentee probably would not have known.

The next stage after explanation is learning by experience. Some people imagine that experience is a delightful teacher. Experience is a painful teacher. Experience is a mean teacher – if I may say so – because it costs you a lot. You can learn through the experiences of others. You are there to watch the consequences of the person's actions. That should be able to release wisdom to you, helping you see the way things shouldn't go. You should also be able to learn from great things that happen.

I celebrate the access God gave me to Pastor E. A. Adeboye, the General Overseer of Redeemed Christian Church of God. What touches me the most is my experience of his humility. The first time I met him physically, I had to drive past his auditorium to meet him in his office. I was humbled by the realisation that I was going past an arena that is more than 1km long, which this man regularly fills to the extent that they are now even struggling for space.

I had the privilege to preach to a group of men of God alongside Daddy G.O (as he is fondly called) at his invitation. To have me preach and teach in his presence while he listened was also very humbling for me. It was just mind-boggling. But the most mind-boggling thing was his humility afterwards. During the break, he got up from his seat, sought me out, put his arms around my shoulders, bowed, and said, '*You really blessed me.*' He then re-preached my message, highlighting what I said that resonated with him, and he was genuinely sincere. When he bowed, I went flat on the floor.

He could see my eyes clouded with tears, and I said, '*Daddy, you are so humble*' And he said to me, '*The higher you go in life and the more successful you become, the greater the demand on you to be humble. Your requirement for your humility increases as God lifts you.*' That shook me to my foundations because what I see around me tends to be the opposite. The moment somebody gets a little more success, they get proud and begin to posture by adding bodyguards, protocols, and the rest.

Daddy G.O's humility is intimidating. I learned from his experience, some of which he shared with me. He has passed through issues so that I don't have to. And all of my mentorship relationships are like that. You will always have more than one mentor. Please don't let anybody deceive you. If God's call upon your life is strategic and valuable, He will constantly add more than one person to you.

You will always have the opportunity to learn. You will learn through your experiences too. The funny thing about life is that sometimes, people are not teachable until adversity happens. It seems like it's until people go through some difficulties, pain, and challenging issues before they are open to learning what they need to know. Pain makes you understand the same thing people have desperately tried to explain earlier.

Adversity forces you to learn. It forces you to know it by force. But the greater level of learning is to be able to learn from the experience of others. And that is what mentorship is all about.

There are some things that only the Holy Spirit can open into your heart.

'But as it is written, Eye hath not seen, nor ear heard, neither have entered into the heart of man, the things which God hath prepared for them that love him. But God hath revealed them unto us by his Spirit: for the Spirit searcheth all things, yea, the deep things of God'. (1 Corinthians 2:9-10 KJV)

Revelation is the work of the Spirit in a man's heart. You will know. There are some things that even your mentor does not know. But the Lord will show you by revelation, and you may not be able to explain it; you simply know it. Revelation is not in the mind; it is in the heart. A person who is accustomed to living his life in the mind will be a person that is not given to revelation. God doesn't cast godly pearls before the swine. It starts in the heart, and then it feeds the mind. We can then understand, and be able to know its ramifications.

So, mentorship should afford us those four portals of learning; observation, explanation, experience, and revelation.

3

Respect Determines Influence

Let me explain an essential principle. If two friends were together, one good and one evil, who would influence the other? The question of who will influence the other is determined by respect. The person who influences is the one that is respected in that relationship. What directs influence is respect; influence flows in the direction of respect. So, respect determines the flow of the anointing. The Bible says; know them that labour among you, esteem them very highly in love for their work sake.

If your pastors are to be effective in your life, respect them. If your leaders are to be effective in your life, respect them. You must choose to lift them so that influence can flow towards you. That's what determines it. Why are parents able to influence their children? Respect is the key. If you take respect out of the equation, you find out that we have very little influence on our children. And that is God's command to us; '*Honor (respect, obey, care for) your father and your mother, so that your days may be prolonged in the land the LORD your God gives you*'. (Exodus 20:12 AMP) So, respect directs influence.

Let me tell you a story to underscore this point I am trying to make. There was a young lawyer who was a bitter guy. He was very brilliant and very straightforward. He came out top in his class with first-class honours, but he was broke. Nobody was giving him cases. Nobody was giving him jobs. He was very bitter because the senior lawyers seemed to be getting more prosperous, and the Junior lawyers were getting poorer. The same people got more and more briefs even though they already had more than enough. One day, this young lawyer went for dinner at one of the law association events and saw one of those senior lawyers kept looking at him and seemed to perceive the disdain and resentment in his heart. This senior lawyer walked toward the young lawyer. Though the senior lawyer was received poorly, he was unperturbed. Undeterred, the senior lawyer gave the young man his card, asking him to meet him in his office by 10 a.m. the next day.

This young lawyer went home, pondered what transpired that night, and decided to visit the old lawyer downtown. When he got to the man's office, the secretary told him that the man had been waiting for him. The senior lawyer got up and told him to come with him. He put his hand on the shoulder of the young lawyer and began to talk about the weather and other trivial issues as they took a stroll. When they got back to the office, the senior lawyer shook hands with the young lawyer and thanked him for accompanying him on the walk. He then made a U-turn, entered his office, and shut the door.

The young man was a bit disappointed, but he started receiving a series of job offers later in the evening. People who had seen him walking with the sage assumed that he must also be gifted to be having such a long discussion with one of the top legal minds. After a series of calls, he realized that the brief contact with the senior lawyer had brought about endless opportunities. Just that single stroll he had with the man had caused his reputation to rub off on him. We profit because we receive an impartation of prestige; it's not just learning by observation, explanation, experience, and revelation. In other words, we benefit from serving.

We also get an impartation of grace and stature due to mentorship. Sometimes, we are oblivious and never even consider rewarding that value because we don't recognize it. I am very mindful of this when I am interacting with young people. I realise that I am imparting my reputation and whatever the Lord has enabled me to achieve through all the years of serving God to the next generation that God is bringing up.

Back to my story, the young lawyer later went back to the senior lawyer, this time with a different attitude – an attitude of gratitude. *'I'm so sorry for how I acted that first night.'* The senior lawyer replied, *'I was as bitter as you were, resentful of those that had gone before me because I thought they had it all easy. And I could recognize that attitude in you. I am so glad that you learnt what you learnt.'* The value of mentorship is that you are blessed to have the privilege to learn by observation, explanation, experience, and revelation. In addition, you get the imparted reputation that comes upon you and propels you far beyond what you imagined doing by yourself. The truth is that this fulfils God's will. He is the One who said, whosoever is faithful in another man's business will be given his own.

4

Three Spiritual Destiny Laws

He that is faithful in that which is least is faithful also in much: and he that is unjust in the least is unjust also in much. (Luke 16:10 KJV)

Laws govern life. God, the giver of life, has set governing rules to guarantee results. This chapter will share three powerful spiritual destiny laws that everyone who seeks to be mentored must understand.

1. Start Small

Start from where you are. Too many people try to start a ministry, for example, with 20 million Naira. I have people who write me letters requesting that they need such a massive sum of money for renting a facility, and so on.

When I started my ministry, my only microphone was my mouth. When we got our first microphone, it was an FM microphone bought for 35 Naira. So to tell me that you need 20 million to start a ministry sounds excessive to me. When I came to Abuja, Nigeria, I went with the same FM microphone to begin the Capital Assembly. I came with what I had. The first spiritual law that governs your destiny is to start from where you are.

God said to Abraham; Abraham, look from where you are and as far as you can see. Before you can see very far, you must know where you are. In other words, use your imagination and be creative but understand where you are. Learn to start; not with what you don't have but with what you have. There is always something that you have. If you say, 'And I don't have capital,' If you look critically, you will discover that you might have favour, connections, and even highly sought after knowledge.

God said to Moses, '*What is in your hand?*' And he said, '*It's a rod, Lord.*' God replied, '*Use that Rod!*' What God will use to bless and multiply you is already within your reach. Just look for it.

2. Put Your Money Where Your Mouth Is

Verse 11 of our opening scripture infers that he that is faithful in unrighteous mammon will be given true riches. Too many people make their budgets based on someone else's pocket. Stop looking for somebody who will help you; look for people to help, and give what you have to them. Stop looking for those who will underwrite your expenses. Get that mentality away from you and put your money where your mouth is. Even banks will not loan you money until they see you commit your own resources to it. NGOs will not invest in you unless you have put in something first.

One of the attributes of leadership is sacrifice. Vision is what makes you a leader, but sacrifice empowers you and makes your leadership legitimate. What have you sacrificed? If you can't sacrifice for your vision or future, you have no right to expect anybody else to sacrifice for it.

3. He that Has Not Been Faithful in Another Man's Own Won't Be Given His Own

This is what is not being taught in Christianity these days. I was called to be an apostle since I gave my life to Christ, but God says, "I'm not going to give you your own until you have been faithful (totally invested in goodness) in another man's own." Many want to graduate and start their own company immediately. Some want to create their ministries as soon as they get born again.

In other words, I will not make you successful until you first make another man successful. I will not bring you into your fruitfulness until someone has become fruitful because of you. Be that Jacob to a Laban and see if the Lord will not go out of His way to shake the earth's foundation for you. It's a spiritual law.

So, these three laws are fundamental, and this third one, in particular, is also something that mentorship forces you to do because it is an exchange of life. This third law is particularly essential, especially when sufficient access is given.

Every mentee should look for opportunities to serve his mentor's vision. What value can you add to your mentor? Don't be a liability, having a general expectation that your mentors should count it a privilege to mentor you. You should rather constantly ask yourself: '*What value am I always adding to this relationship?*'

Sometimes, God must open the door of perception for you to be able to add value. Let me give you an example. I have a mentor based in the U.S. I remember the first time I stepped into his church. Oh my God! Talk about the secrets of my heart being made manifest. He got up, turned to me, and said, '*I know you are not from here, and you came into the States, but I will prophesy into your destiny.*' I hadn't even been introduced to him at the time, and he just started sharing and pouring out deep things God had been speaking to me.

I was on the floor, rolling and crying like a baby. After that, God joined our hearts together. I later asked him, '*How can I serve you, sir? I am a pastor. I am a man of God, and I pastor pastors.*' I do a lot in the area of media. I pointed out to him that I once trained the person who was his media director at the time. I humbly offered my services. The bishop didn't know any of these things about me. He refused my offer because his perception of me had not yet opened that service door for me. However, I refused to give up and kept looking for other ways to serve because I wouldn't let somebody be adding value to my life like he was doing, and I wouldn't add value in return.

So, I started looking for ways that I could serve him. The first thing I did was find out how to get his bank account number. I made up my mind to start giving. I put money aside, put it in an envelope, and after meeting with him on many occasions, I handed him that envelope in one of those meetings.

Bishop took the envelope from me, prayed, and put it down. Graciously, he received it but didn't open the envelope and then continued speaking, sharing and teaching from his heart. That's another thing that I learned from him as a mentee; he did not open it in my presence. No matter what it is; and who it is, I no longer open gifts in the giver's presence unless specifically requested. I now receive each gift the same way, and I pray from the depths of my heart as if I have received a million dollars.

Still, my heart was yearning; what are the other ways I could help this man? So, I said to him, '*I'd like to come over to the house. I would like to help with your laundry. I would like to polish your shoes.*' I deliberately put myself in that position because I wanted to return value and receive the blessing from serving him. You receive the anointing of mentors when you serve them. Serving opens doors and engages the anointing.

Let me give you an example. I usually use the story of Jacob to explain compassion. Isaac asked Esau to hunt an animal in the bush for him so that he could bless him. When I saw those words, "so that I may bless you," I pondered the relationship between the "meat" and the "blessings". Is there any spiritual connection between venison stew and the anointing?

I then understood that the true power of blessing rests upon God, the source of that blessing. Compassion is a key to God's anointing. Isaac was looking for a way to connect with God so he could bless his son, knowing that in that connection with God, the blessing would indeed be effective.

Esau went hunting and came back late. Rebecca had called Jacob and told him to go and kill a lamb, prepare food and give it to his father to receive the blessing. He did precisely that, and the father ate it and was happy. He was emotionally moved by it. I always tell people that your emotions are the amplifier of the voice of your spirit. That's the God-designed purpose of your emotions. So, if you are safe, your emotions will amplify it with peace and joy beyond explanation. If you enter a place and feel uncomfortable, your emotions boost it because something is threatening in that place. So, your emotion is also a gateway to your heart.

When the food pleased Isaac so much, his spirit opened, and he blessed Jacob. When Esau eventually showed up, Isaac told Esau, *"I have blessed your brother when you left; he came, and I blessed him, and he is* **blessed indeed...** *I have sustained him."* He spoke in the past tense of a future event that was yet to happen. Imagine that! The man was about to die, yet he said I 'have' sustained him with bread and wine. That meant he would never be poor and suffer lack. He talked about what would happen in the future as if it had already happened. That is the power of the blessing. Blessing secures what will happen in the future. And this happened all because Isaac was well pleased. There is a trigger to every blessing and anointing.

Elisha was known as a prophet that served another prophet. We miss that a lot today. God opens opportunities for service and possibilities of lifting. John Maxwell is a man whose story and the testimony he shares show that he has a heart of service that has opened the door for him again and again. John wrote letters to many ministers he greatly admired, requesting just 30 minutes of their time by offering to take them out for lunch. Also, he has a culture of placing a $100 note in an envelope and handing it to them after their time together to appreciate them. That is the heart of service. It **is** not about money. It's about rewarding value. It is about unlocking a key of compassion in the heart of a mentor.

5

Maximising A Mentee-Mentor Relationship

People enter into mentoring relationships and have massive expectations of their mentor. They want their mentor to be always available and always involved in anything they are doing. They also wish their mentor could love them unconditionally, etc. Sometimes people never ask about the expectations of a mentee from a mentor in a mentoring relationship. The tendency is to have a lot of expectations.

There is an added expectation of bankrolling in Nigeria, from where I come. When people say you are their father or mentor, they begin to make their plans and budget their projects based on your resources, not theirs. They think if you are their mentor, you ought to support them financially. I used to believe that when people were telling me about their projects, they wanted counsel and wisdom, but I have found out that most are simply looking for money. That is a gross abuse of a mentorship relationship.

While you have expectations of your mentor, please realise that you can't control how your mentor behaves or what he does, but you can control what you do. Instead of having expectations of your mentor, have expectations of yourself. You must understand and discern the normal expectations you are required to have as a mentee.

1. Honour

I have mentioned this earlier, honour determines the flow of influence. Honour is the key that determines the direction of influence.

2. Service

Bishop T.D. Jakes articulates this in better words than I have ever done. He said, 'The anointing doesn't fall on you by prayer; the anointing falls on you through service'. If you see someone who is very good at something you want to be good at, you don't just stroll to that person so they can lay hands on you, and then what is upon them will be upon you. It never happens that way. The key to it is serving. Every mentee must be wise enough to creatively discern the opportunities to serve when you are in the presence of your mentor.

Service is what attracts the anointing, appropriates grace, and transfers the supernatural from that person to you. There are many ways that you can serve. You can serve by encouraging them. You can serve by actually alleviating some physical burdens that they carry. You can serve by sowing seeds – giving, not erratically but solidly. You can serve by being available to help. Do you remember the story of Elijah and Elisha? The Bible says they could tell that this man was anointed. Why? Because he was the one that poured water on the hands of Elijah. So, every time Elijah was going to eat, Elisha would be there to pour water on his hands.

Look at Jesus and His disciples. A story says that Jesus commanded His disciples to go to the other side. Then he was in the boat with them, asleep as they rowed. Jesus was recuperating all the energy expended in preaching, laying hands, and meeting the expectations of people, a burden that people seem not to understand that mentors carry. But when He was in the boat, He was sleeping while they were rowing. When they were in the storm, He was asleep. They woke Him up and said, "Can't you see that we will perish? Don't you care?" They probably imagined that having to row the boat while He was resting was terrible, but it was an opportunity of service for them and serving invokes a blessing.

Small keys open big doors. Honour is the key that ushers the flow of influence in your direction, but serving is the key that unleashes that anointing. You can even tap into another person's anointing without that person's will when you serve them accurately. I know of people who have been devoted to giving to a specific man of God, and they would also get on their knees and pray for him. They thus served as intercessors without the person even knowing that they were on their intercessory team. Benny Hinn is one of such people. I recently saw a picture on social media where they had cropped out a photo of Benny Hinn in one of his colourful poses while ministering. They combined it with a picture of Kathryn Kuhlman, also ministering. It was done to make it appear like the two were ministering side by side.

I knew that was photoshopped because Benny Hinn never got the chance to stand on the same pulpit with Kathryn Kuhlman, as he testified. However, what is true is that he sounds like her and ministers like her. The same anointing that flowed through her flows through him.

How did that happen? He served Kathryn Kuhlman's ministry after she died. He had attended a few of her meetings, but he really had the chance to help after she died. He was always available for them. He preached for them, and he wouldn't want to receive any remuneration because he saw it as an opportunity to serve.

One of the things he did while she was still alive was getting and coordinating buses to bring people from whatever town he was into whatever town she was ministering to, and she never knew about it. So, it's not as if she chose him as the one that will carry the mantle of the grace of God upon her life when she was gone. He served his way into it. That option is open to every one of us.

When we are in a mentorship relationship, we should look for every opportunity to create opportunities to serve. Talking about my mentor, the Bishop, again, I remember God opened massive doors for him before he went to be with the Lord. He was often in the White House, and he was on TBN, Daystar, and featured in Time Magazine. He was also once on the cover of Charisma magazine. God had opened massive doors for him. I remember the first time I met him and said, *"Bishop, please allow me to come to the house. I would love to help you with your laundry, ironing, and shoes. When I am at home in Nigeria, I am the General Overseer, and faithful helpers surround me, but here, I only want an opportunity to serve you."* But the man simply smiled.

He didn't initially offer me that opportunity, so I started looking for those opportunities myself. He didn't give me those opportunities but would rather spend time with me over dinner or lunch, but I was desperate for those opportunities.

He said to me one day, *'I would love you to preach in church next Sunday,'* and I said this is my opportunity. I went and prepared. My wife was pregnant at that time, and we would have the baby in the U.S. The bill for the delivery came to about

$12,000, and it was at that time, that he gave me the opportunity to minister in his amazing church. All that was in my heart was, how can I serve this man?. I could see what was going on in the church and the trends, and I yearned for God to use me to help. I opened my heart to God, and when I got on that pulpit, help was precisely what God enabled me to deliver. It was something he couldn't do for himself, someone had to do it for him, and I allowed God to use me to bring help.

I remember him asking if he could have my account details so that the church could put the honorarium, but I refused because it was my chance to give back to him by serving. Even though I was desperate for the money at the time, I wouldn't receive it. He asked me to go to the church office to receive it, and they presented it to me. Without even looking at the amount, I declined it. I remember his daughter exclaiming, '*Wow! You are from Nigeria, and you reject an American church offering?*'

That was the most prominent church I had ministered in at the time. I just needed opportunities to serve, and I genuinely wanted to help in any way that I could. I used the opportunity to serve my mentor, and I promised that I was always willing to serve whenever I was around.

When I did that, Bishop took me seriously. The following week he said, '*I am going to New York, and I would like you to come with me*' I explained that I had issues with my mobility, and he said I should not worry that he had that covered. I showed up in the office and escorted him as his armour bearer on one of his trips to go and preach at TBN.

He didn't know I was studying to start our satellite broadcast station. I was looking to understand the operations behind the scene and all of that. That trip was such a blessing and inspiration to me. I wasn't just an armour bearer; my heart and eyes were open to learning exactly how the network did the lighting, prepped people before broadcast, and how they made the backdrops. I had the opportunity to meet amazing people too. I wasn't there trying to project myself, I was just there as the armour-bearer, but God kept drawing people's attention. I met ministers who were also ministering on TBN and so on. Service triggers the anointing. Look for a way to serve if you want anything to come upon you.

One of the ways you can serve your mentor, which is vital, is encouragement. That affirmation that you think you need, your mentor needs even more. Jesus healed ten lepers, but only one returned to give thanks. That is the reality of life. Only one will return to affirm you for every ten people you bless and every ten people's lives you touch.

I married the best woman God could ever have given to me in my life. Even when I preached and nobody came back to say anything, my wife would come back, and she would always preach my messages to me and encourage me. It is scarce that my wife would not say anything. I am of all men most fortunate. I often wonder if she knows how nourishing it is because the ratio of those who come back to affirm me is 1:10. It was so with Jesus, and it will be so with us. It's just the nature of ministry. Create a way to serve by encouraging your mentor. Encouragement is a service.

If you discern who your mentor is, you should be able to encourage them more accurately. Pastors thrive best in personal interaction or direct coaching, and the teacher thrives when passing across the knowledge. If a person's call or usefulness is in teaching the Word, an attentive listener is the best encouragement that person can ever receive. You would be on point and stand out from the crowd if you do that. If the person is a motivator, it would be immensely nourishing to him if you become highly motivated due to their input. If you discern your mentor, you will understand the primary platform for delivering that encouragement and open yourself to that. That person will so fall in love with you.

Don't give unsolicited advice to your mentor, no matter the situation. When your mentor asks you what you think, usually what they are hoping is that you would encourage them. I have asked people what they think, and I got a full-fledged lecture from a critical spirit. When I ask what you think, I usually seek affirmation that you got what I was trying to pass across.

Let me share a personal experience with a mentor in the early stages of my formation with you. I did music theory in secondary school, so I sang in the choir. I had a wonderful woman who encouraged my ability in that regard. When I was in the university, I heard a minister that blew my mind. I eventually had the privilege of serving under his brother. He was the choir leader in the church I attended. He had his itinerant ministry and would travel worldwide, but he was also the music director in our home church, and I was the bass guitarist. I had the privilege of understanding him in terms of his music. My first two albums were recorded in his studio.

I would go there, sit and learn. I got all my knowledge of sound engineering from him. As far as music and sound engineering were concerned, he was my mentor. I used 'was' because I no longer have proximity to him. As our relationship developed, I noticed that he would always come to me when the Lord gave him a new song so I could tell him what I thought. He would ask me to listen, and I would listen and tell him what I didn't like or criticised the song. I did that every time.

Even though I thought what I was saying was important, necessary, and sound, it created the opposite effect. He would become deflated and smile, but those songs would never be released. There was this particular one that he didn't release for ten years until I told him that the song was one of the best songs I had ever heard from him. I told him that I wanted to have it? I desired to put it in my album if he didn't want to use it'. He felt encouraged and released it in his next album. I then began to understand my role in encouraging him.

Then it dawned on me that each time he came to say '*What do you think?*', he wasn't looking for my criticism; he was looking for my affirmation. Whenever a mentor asks you what you think, please be careful. He doesn't need your criticism, he needs your affirmation. We often criticise because we try to impress our mentors with our knowledge or aptitude. Your mentor is already impressed with you.

When I learned that key, I practised it with every other mentor who came to me. At a point, he noticed I was no longer offering criticism. Whenever he came to me, I would not only provide affirmation, but I would also start playing the song repeatedly, immediately. I also ensured he saw me playing the music, and I would also share them with other people.

He would later say, 'Thank you for your encouragement, but I also need your ideas and input because they are quite beneficial'. So, I had to find a way to give those corrections in an affirming manner. It was more nourishing. It has become palatable, and it is now delivered in a manner that doesn't crush the person.

When you set someone up as being your giver, nourisher, and provider, you, the mentee, will never see yourself in the position of giving or reciprocating. The Bible says he who has been ministered to in spiritual gifts should always respond and reciprocate in kind and value. If the person ministers spiritual things, reply and return with material items. If the person gives you advice, don't reciprocate by providing a piece of advice; reciprocate by giving the person another kind of blessing.

Shortly after I rejected the offering in Bishop's church, I went to preach in another church in New York, and they gave me a massive gift. The gift was so enormous in my eyes, but the Lord said I should give it to my Bishop again. It was a very awkward situation.

I had rejected an offering, and I was returning with another gift as the Lord was leading me to do. The man was amazed, which changed his perception of Nigerians as a people. He spoke a blessing over my life, and I left. The best part of the testimony is that the hospital wrote off the twelve thousand dollar bill for the delivery of our child because I was obedient to God. God is faithful!

1. Shut Up

You can't talk and listen simultaneously, and the hearing benefits you more. Be quicker to hear than to speak. In a mentoring relationship, be quicker to listen. One of the things that really blessed my heart about Dr Samuel Ekundayo, which was why I could be myself around him, is his spiritual sensitivity. We could be joking and having fun, but he would ask me a billion questions and sense it when I switch into the spirit and start to prophesy. Many people don't have the grace for that when they get familiar with their mentor. They don't understand that some of the things you say with a smile on your face and laughter in your tone were prophetic utterances from God. Some people can't discern when something spiritual occurs, which is very bad.

In mentorship, you will see the person in the spirit and the flesh, and you can learn from both. You can learn from someone's mistakes as much as you can learn from someone's successes. In a mentorship relationship, you are exposed to both sides. The more profound mentorship is, the closer you are to both ends of the spectrum, and you should be able to discern and know what to pick up and what to drop.

God will tell you, '*This is your immunization jab against lust*', or '*This is your immunization jab against greed*' because you had seen it play out before and noticed its effects. You are sensitive to it because of your exposure to your mentor. You have seen both sides of the coin, so you now know how to shut this door because you have seen how it can creep in so easily. You have seen the bad, the good, and the ugly. But that ability to be sensitive to know when this person is prophesying, when this person is serious or joking, and to honour the person still is a treasure for any mentee.

One of the things I have learned as a mentor is that I shouldn't have an opinion on every matter. Most times, if people are chit-chatting, I mostly shut down. I don't do too much chit-chatting because those around me will find it challenging to know when I speak from the Lord if I chat a lot about everything. If I keep talking about what Lionel Messi should be doing, what Bill Clinton should have done, and constantly babbling, it will be more challenging to discern when I speak under unction from the Lord.

There are two kinds of people who come to me for prayers; one set of people claim to be there for prayer, yet for 15 minutes, they are going on and on about what and how I should pray. The second simply says, 'Pray for me', and almost every time I open my mouth, it becomes prophetic, and God speaks to me about certain things happening in their lives. This kind of manifestation of God becomes even more powerful because it builds their faith to realise that this is supernatural; otherwise, how could I have known? Be more ready to listen than to speak. Speak less, listen more; it's vital for a mentee. Just shut up and listen, observe and learn.

Also, if you are in a mentorship relationship, it's not a classroom. Some people don't benefit from a mentorship relationship because they are best in a traditional classroom where a teacher comes to class, tells you his topic, and starts teaching. That is how they prefer to learn. When you are exposed to somebody who is a mentor, you should constantly be observing, and you shouldn't just switch off or put your brain on reverse. It is better not to have dinner with your mentor, and all your focus is on the potatoes and how the chicken is not done right.

You could even learn something from how your mentor responds to the waiters and staff when you are tuned in. You grow by asking questions that only pop up when you are a good listener, observant, and not too quick to speak or too eager to show up and dominate the conversation. Be calm and learn.

The exciting thing about learning is what isn't always heard. What determines what you hear is often the need in your life. You are more sensitive to picking things because there is a need in your life. That is another area where one needs to be careful. Certain things will be said that you don't need right now, and you might shut it down. You shouldn't let your attention span discard them. Don't discard anything; keep it. The Bible said about Joseph's father that he kept it in his heart though he did not understand Joseph's dream.

Let me give you an example. I went to preach in Lagos. I can't remember if it was my meeting or someone else's meeting, but I was the speaker. This guy seated in the congregation used to work as the manager in a printing press. Then, the Lord began to speak through me in the word of knowledge to different people. It was so supernatural, so this guy could tell that God was using me. Then I called his name, pointed at him, and said, 'Wale, the Lord tells me you will *own a satellite TV station*'. The guy sat down and was wondering what a joker I was. He had in his heart that things were not going well in his job as a printing press manager, and he really wanted to keep his career, but here I was talking of owning a satellite TV station. I further said, '*Come, if you believe it, let me lay hands on you*' He sat where he was because it was so farfetched but not to embarrass me, he came out, and the Lord said to him through me, '*Be faithful in little. The faithfulness in the little things will open this grace upon your life*'.

I didn't even remember until a year later when this man called me and said, '*Bishop, I want you to send me every message you have ever preached in your life. I want you to send it to me, and I will put it on my satellite station'*. I was surprised, so I asked him what had happened? He explained that he'd been struggling to keep his job when I prophesied way outside his comfort zone and expectation. To cut a long story short, someone came to do a job, saw his attitude, and said he would like him to run their printing press. He moved to the new guy's printing press, and my words kept replaying in his head, *'Your faithfulness in little things…'*.

Soon after, the new boss said to him, *'We have this satellite broadcasting network, and I would love for you to manage it'* He explained that he had never managed one before, but the guy's response was, *'It's not a problem, I will teach you everything you need to know'*. That was how he became the manager of the satellite station. He understudied the guy for about six months and understood what it takes. The guy then further explained that he was planning to shut the thing down but seeing how he had handled it, he would no longer shut it down but instead offer him ownership of the satellite network. This offer included the registration, the accreditation, equipment and everything. That was how he gave the man every single thing free of charge. The boss said he could see his heart and how he was especially good at it. That is amazing.

I am uncomfortable when people around me are too spooky and spiritualise everything. Have the sensitivity to know when someone begins to speak by the Spirit. Some people require a formal classroom setting to learn and move forward. Still, others are mature, quiet, observant, slow to speak, and quick to hear to benefit from a mentorship relationship.

Sometimes, mentors will say something you disagree with or don't understand. Just keep it in the corner of your heart. Some people are too contentious. You don't have to say it every time you don't agree with something. It's unnecessary to argue because you don't know where God is taking that conversation. Those are things I will advise any mentee to do to make relating with their mentor effective.

Abuse of mentorship

I think the worst abuse of mentorship is often from the mentor. Mentorship could be abused as the annexation of the mentee. Spiritual colonising involves setting the mentee up to serve you for your ego and certain benefits. Those benefits could be reputation, finances, etc.

Mentorship is never about you. If you are mentoring someone and it's always about you, even the mentee will eventually tire of that relationship and want out. But if it is unto the Lord and the person's destiny as designed by God, that is a different ball game altogether.

The abuse from the mentee's side is that the mentee becomes selfish and thinks that it is about him/her alone. It is about the will of God. One of the most significant abuses I see in mentees is that they fail to understand what the relationship is about and what it means. So many people come into a relationship they term as mentorship, and all they truly want is another fan.

Every one of us desires affirmation and admiration. There is something about assurance and esteem that encourages and keeps us motivated, so we all long for it. But that longing can quickly become distorted. I keep telling people that your penny can make you blind to the pounds beyond it if you put it too close to your eye. It's not that penny is not good, but it obscures the blessings around you.

When all you want is affirmation and someone who will always applaud you, you break the chain of a mentorship relationship. Every time you come into that person's presence, trying to tell them, *'This is what I have done'*, or *'This is who I am'*, wanting to impress them, fishing for applause, you will miss God's wisdom.

This principle is one of many things I have learnt from my mentors. In the earlier part of our relationships, I often felt insecure and wanted them to know who I was. I was always trying to impress them. I wasn't competing; I was fishing for affirmation. I wanted them to think highly of me. That was unnecessary because we wouldn't even have been in those mentorship relationships if they weren't already impressed with me. When mentors give you access to their lives, works, and all else, it is an evidence that they are already impressed with you. So, being the one doing the talking most of the time, telling all my stories whenever we were together, and throwing my accomplishments around, made me miss much of the wisdom God had placed in my early mentors.

While wisdom passes both ways in a mentorship relationship, the direction of influence is predominantly from the mentor to the mentee. It would help if you didn't get so busy trying to impress that you miss out on what your mentor has to offer.

The Bible says, *'Iron sharpeneth iron; so a man sharpeneth the countenance of his friend'* (Proverbs 27:17), so we infer that influence is a currency that is constantly flowing. Either I am influencing you, or you are influencing me; it's one of the two. It's never stagnant. Influence is continually flowing. People say if you want to know what a person will become in five years, look at the people they have surrounded themselves with now. That could be true and false. It is true. After all, influence has to happen, and wrong because something can determine the direction of the influence. Jesus was with his disciples, yet He wasn't turning out to become like them; they were becoming like Him.

So, the influence has to be directional, and honour determines the direction of influence in any relationship. You attract what you respect and pull towards what you esteem. It's like water. Water flows (downwards) towards the force of gravity. Honour determines the direction of influence. What you honour and you are impressed with, you become. So, when you are in a mentorship relationship and constantly trying to impress the person, you shut the door of influence to yourself. It has to be the other way around; you should continually look for what to be impressed with, not criticise. When you are in the presence of mentors, you should show enthusiasm for their wisdom and experiences. That way, you turn the key of influence to flow in the right direction. Remember that mentorship is about getting you from where you are to where God wants you to be.

6

The Mentorship Process

I believe that there should be a process to mentorship, and those four gateways to learning that I mentioned earlier in chapter 2 should help strengthen the process. However, an undergirding principle must be embraced first – Everybody should not have an equal right of access to you. The Bible says a man with no control over his spirit is like a city without walls (Proverbs 25:28). Even among Jesus' disciples, there were the inner three that he would take with him on a few occasions while the other nine waited. So, everybody did not have equal access.

That attitude where you feel as if you were entitled to equal access or that the person would be available to you on-demand is not correct. If you look very well into scripture, there was not a single one of Jesus' disciples that chose Jesus. Jesus chose all of them. He went to each of them and said, '*Follow me*'. If you look at the life of Jesus, most of the people who came to Jesus and said, *I want to follow you*, He redirected and said, '*No, go back.*' And there were those he called who were not ready to pay the sacrifice like the Rich Young Ruler at that time, but generally, nobody made it into Jesus' inner circle that he, himself, didn't make the final decision to let them in. He called them, but they didn't call him. I hope you understand that.

So, he even said in the scripture, "*I chose you.*" Every mentor has the right to choose the people he mentors. It's not a God-given right. So, you must always see it as a privilege when somebody gives you access and proximity and recognize that you should do what you can to earn it. Of course, it's God's favour to open that door for you, but please return value by doing your best to earn it. Earn it with your honour. Earn it with the attitude of your heart. Earn it with your reciprocation of value in whatever way the Lord enables you to do, and most importantly, earn it by your confidentiality. When God gives you the privilege of a true mentor, and there is an exchange of life, you'll see the person in their worst moments and their best moments.

The undergirding principle I have talked about shows that there must be a hierarchy. You cannot mentor everybody at the same level. I realized that I could not mentor better than Jesus, and I realized that Jesus chose 12 to be his inner circle, the ones that went with him to wherever he went. He couldn't handle more than 12. So I'll be foolhardy to think I can mentor 500 people as Jesus mentored his 12. So there must be a certain number of people you can genuinely handle in your inner circle.

There are people that I call if I don't hear from them. It will be strange to these people if I am not in touch with them for one week, two weeks, three weeks, or one month. For instance, Dr Sam falls in that category. If he doesn't call me, I call him. However, that's not for everyone. Everybody can't be in that position.

Know that the hierarchy will also involve methods of execution of your mentorship. Some people call me to say, "*I would like you to mentor me.*" And I will say, "*Fantastic! Let's start that mentorship with your exposure to my materials. I will give you the contact to the person who runs our bookstore. I'll give you the person's contact details who handles my resources and materials.*" I may say, "*There's a book I wrote,*" for some. "*It is called The Making of Chosen Vessel. I'd like you to start reading from chapter 9. There is something I wrote in chapter 9 that I believe will be important to your life and everything.*"

It's a test. Don't mentor anybody who is not willing to stretch to reach you. Pursuit is the evidence of desire. The mentee should be ready to commit to and want your mentorship. You can't effectively mentor anybody at their convenience. It won't work. Like the Rich Young Ruler, some people would immediately ask or insinuate, *"Do you know who I am? Why should I go and buy your books? I am talking about mentorship, and you are talking about books."*

Meanwhile, it is a test. Let's see you reach for that first. Let's see how far you get. Imagine what it's like when somebody comes to you and says, *"Sir, I was listening to your message. This message so blessed me as I was listening to this or that."*

Let me cite the example of a friendship that recently happened. Dr Samuel engineered my connection with a friend of his. Before the man met me, he had already diligently gone to look me up on social media to study what I was doing. The fellow knew where my church was. He had started listening to my messages. Wow! By the time we were meeting for the first time, he was already telling me, *"I love how you do this and that."* That endeared my heart to him. His action automatically opened the wealth of compassion in my heart. I immediately felt I would love to know him much better.

In a mentorship, there are different levels of hierarchy. There are people that I mentor through my materials. There are others that I mentor in a big group. Then, there are people that I mentor personally. Jesus could not mentor everybody personally in His earthly walk. Only a few walked with him, ate, slept on the same boat, etc. Not everyone can access that.

There is another fallacy that I would like to address about mentorship. Going back to where we started in chapter one, Mentor was to groom the young man, Telemachus, to become the next king. Mentor was not a king. The erroneous idea that some folk have been either spreading or propagating is that people must have some prominence before they can function as mentors. Sometimes we begin to look down on our mentors the moment one or two successes happen in our lives. That is so myopic and so sad.

Mentor was never going to be a king. It was not his calling. Yet, it was his job to bring up this young man to become king. Every mentor may not necessarily be in the same position you will be. They are exposed to so many different dimensions, and there are things in their lives that God feels are necessary for your future. That is why God calls us together. Learn to celebrate them and be humble. God will bring people to you.

God will bring wealthy people and people who are not rich and expect them to mentor you. He will bring you to famous people and those who are not well-known, and he expects them too to mentor you. Mentors might address your marriage, and their lives would serve as an icon in that area. Others may be acting as icons in Ministries and Business and may be very different from the previous. Nobody is perfect in everything. God doesn't invest everything into one person; He invests in all his children. You must have a humble heart and the ability to listen to God rather than reason things out in your head. The Bible says that the companion of fools shall be destroyed. Don't apply that beyond the original intention and use it as a means of disqualifying mentors that God is sending to you.

You need a few people in your life that will teach you to have your foot on the ground. A few people in your life who are not interested in your fame, money, or clout are grounded enough to keep you humble. You need a few people to do that. Avoid that attitude of wanting to be with the in-crowd. The hustler's mentality is that everybody is looking for popular hyper-achievers. They are not the only people qualified to mentor you. That is not how God wants it to be.

Take a look at the Scriptures, and you will find that God caused kings to be mentored by prophets. The king of Israel called out to the prophet, Elisha, "My father, shall I smite them," even though the prophet had nothing compared to the king's wealth and riches (2nd Kings 20:21). Every king needs a seer. Also, let's not be too cerebral; you might need to be mentored by a few people who have failed before. Since they have tasted that failure, you can learn from their pain.

You cannot give what you do not have. It takes wisdom to mentor. If you recognize that mentorship is discipleship, you must have had an encounter with the person you are moulding your disciple to become. For instance, somebody who has worked as a Managing Director of one of Aliko Dangote's many companies has likely had direct exposure to Dangote – how he thinks and acts. Sometimes, senior staff in the management or even his special assistant could mentor you better than Dangote himself.

If you look at the story of Esther and the king, the difference between Queen Esther and all the other women that were tested with the same opportunity that made Esther the queen is something most people do not recognize. It's not because she was more beautiful or what she wore. Esther was not the only one who had the privilege of one night with the king and could ask for anything. But, she was the only one that respected the eunuch enough to ask what she would need. The eunuch knew the king and understood his desires. Every other person gave their own opinion about what they wanted, and they failed. Esther trusted the wisdom and the counsel of the one who had lived his whole life in the king's service. It was an act of humility to defer to his insight on Esther's part.

Getting a mentor should be by the leading of the Almighty God, and it should be with the heart of humility. So, I guess everybody can mentor somebody if they have encountered Jesus and had exposure to the future that person is heading towards in one aspect or the other. That qualifies them.

As prominent and successful as Bishop David Oyedepo is, he has a mentor. As mighty as the Lord had made him, he was not ashamed to say, *"Kenneth Copeland mentors me."* I attended Bishop Oyedepo's bible school in 1987. I happened to have been in the second set that graduated from his bible school.

I believe in the law of sowing and reaping. Rather than arrogate glory to yourself, learn to sow honour, and you shall also reap honour. Show respect to others, and you will reap respect. Too few men of God are surrounded by humility, no pride, and no negative attitude or disposition.

If everybody calls you father and nobody calls you son, you've got a problem. If everybody calls you teacher and you are not a student anywhere, you've got some issues.

Remember to be careful as a mentor. Don't give everybody the same level of access. Some words guide me, such as, *"let them first be proved."* It would help if you didn't make anybody a Deacon or an Apostle suddenly; **let them first be proved**. That's very important. Let there be a filtration process. Not everyone who calls you Lord is saying it from the heart. Like it was when Paul gathered a bunch of sticks with a serpent hidden within, everything seemed fine. The moment he set down the bunch of twigs into the fire, the snake struck. You will never know what is in men's hearts until pressure or persecution comes, you make a mistake or fall. You may never know. All kinds of people may surround you, but let there be some fire first. Put some fire around the people you would like to give access to you. Test them first.

I have learnt this lesson the hard way. I have been bitten several times. It's only by the grace of God that the poison of the viper has not affected me permanently or scarred me beyond recognition. So, what I'm sharing with you is from deep experience, and I can tell you that even from the experience of my mentors. Don't be too quick to give everyone total access. Let them first be proved.

We Should Always Prove Them First

I say this to the mentors and also to the mentees. Paul says, 'Prove them first, and then you can put them in the office'. He remarked that deacons should have a good report and recommendations before being put in higher office. Prove them first. Don't put anybody into a position or give them access to your life until they have proven themselves.

Look at the only woman called 'the wise woman' in scripture. We didn't even know her name. We didn't know much about her except that she was wise. The wisdom showed itself when she saw a prophet passing by; that was Elijah. She went to her husband and said, *'Let us invite him for lunch, let him eat with us while he is going on this trip'*. After eating with them and conducting himself decently, she now goes to the husband and asks, *'Can we give him a room in our house'*.

In other words, she tested him at the dining table before she brought him into her house. That is wisdom. We should develop ways of discerning a minister's heart and motives before committing to long-term giving. We should recognize opportunities presented as tests, and so many possibilities come that way because God wants to open greater doors.

We don't only prove our disciples; we also test our mentors. I am not asking you to be critical or judgmental. You should, however, want to verify that the person's heart is right and indeed towards you and the will of God for your life, so prove them first. Trust in the Lord, but prove men. Don't enter into any relationship without firsthand experience and interaction with the other person. Let that trust lead you to take specific steps, and it is vital.

Control the access to your life and your heart. Submit everything to God but remember that He will allow you to prove them first. Even God says that about himself, *'Prove ye Me now... if I will not open the windows of heaven to thee...'* (Malachi 3:10). God encourages us to put Him to the test, but God doesn't expect us to be perpetually testing Him and never trusting Him. So, don't be like that.

Somebody once shared this testimony about me, saying, *'Bishop Bob is a man of God.'* He started listing very terrible things he had done to me. *'I wish you knew all the things I did to provoke him. I did this, and I did that'.*

This man was a manager at the hotel we hosted our church services. He was furious about Christianity, and he just wanted to prove that all men of God were charlatans. He kept on doing nasty things. We would book the hall for service by 8 a.m., and by 7 a.m., he would pour beer on the carpet of the room that we were to use. He would light like five or six cigarettes so that the smoke would fill the air deliberately. He would also erratically move us from room to room at the last minute, and he knew we would have to set up all our equipment.

Sometimes we would come to make our payments, and he would say the place was already booked, while in reality, we had booked many weeks in advance. We would then ask if he could give us an alternative because we had already advertised that venue, but He would insist that nowhere else was available unless we wanted to use the garden or the car park.

This guy eventually gave his life to Christ and is now a very successful minister in the UK. He testified before his congregation as he brought me up to preach. He recounted all these things, which I never knew he did. He mentioned them because he wanted to use the opportunity to repent before his entire church, and then he laid prostrate on the floor, asking for my forgiveness and requesting that I should please say a blessing over him. He kept on saying that I am a true man of God.

When I got up there, I prayed for him and blessed him, but I confessed before the people that I was not sure I passed his test. I didn't know how, but for some reasons, God made me blind to everything that he did because if I had known, I probably would have misbehaved. I couldn't take the credit, and I thanked God because it wasn't for my goodness. I think God just put a blindfold on my eyes, so I didn't see any of his actions, and that was why I didn't respond to them. I probably would have been upset.

What I am saying is don't overdo it, don't over-test. Learn to trust, but don't throw your trust at someone you don't know. First, let them win that trust by the test, then submit to them in a trusting relationship. If you keep perpetually testing and never trusting, you lose.

7

Mentorship Levels and Management

There are different levels of mentorship. If you look closely at Jesus and his disciples in Matthew Chapter 26, you will see different levels of mentorship, all climaxing in the picture-perfect mentorship of all. Let's break them down:

1. Those who will eat from you.

In verse 20 of that chapter, the Bible talks about Jesus gathering his disciples to eat. That is level 1 – The people who will eat with you, the people who will eat your life's fruit. The fruit of our lives is what our lives produce from which other people draw benefits. So, people who come to benefit from you are the first level of mentorship. You don't despise or reject the people. God has ordained that such people will get around you because of the fruit your life supplies, the need you meet, and its value in their lives. That is the shallowest level of mentorship. When the food dries, their mentorship terminates.

2. Those who will bear fruit with you

By Verse 30, the Bible says, 'They went out to the Mount of Olives'. Olive is a kind of fruit. They went beyond eating with Him to bearing fruit with Him. There will be people whose lives you trigger. They are those that you influence. You catalyze their lives and enable them to bear fruit.

3. Those who can be offended by you

In verse 31, Jesus told them that they would be offended because of Him, and Peter said that was not possible. Then Jesus warned him that he would deny Him three times before the cock crowed. Jesus made a powerful statement, '*You all will be offended because of me, but when I have risen…*'. In other words, when I have risen is when you'll be restored. That means the offence will not be permanent. You have to get a certain level of mentorship where you survive offences.

Mentorship that cannot survive transgression is shallow. There are some people you will offend, yet it does not terminate your relationship. There are others you will offend, and that is it. Jesus was with His disciples and told them I would upset you by dying, you will not understand why, and you will all scatter. It is a deep level of mentorship that survives offence.

I had this person I thought knew me so well and was in tune with my ministry until I came down with COVID. I used the opportunity of my illness to publicly address those who believed that COVID didn't exist and that it was all a conspiracy theory. Others said that Bill Gates created it because he was the Antichrist, and they had all sorts of ideas about it. There was also a scenario where ministers hid their challenges and intimidated their followers with statements like '*I can never be sick*', but the Bible tells us the opposite. It says, *"If any be sick among you."* and that '*Many are the afflictions of the righteous, But the LORD delivers him out of them all*'. God doesn't give us a life free of challenges. He provides us with the cure to overcome those challenges.

So by making myself open about my illness, I offended this person. He felt I shouldn't have let people know. I had neutralised his false notion about faith, and he thought I was a bad example. That was it! This person shut me down and cancelled me altogether. As a result, I realised that the relationship was far shallower than I had assumed. There is a level of mentorship that survives offence. You don't throw unfettered access to anybody you have not yet offended. If our relationship is not strong enough to heal from an infraction, I should limit your access to my life and the secrets I expose to you.

4. Those you will leave behind at Gethsemane

Gethsemane is a compound word that means 'Crushing of grapes'. Gethsemane is the winepress of oil from the Mount of Olives. It is a place where the olives are crushed so that the oil will come out of them.

There is a price to pay for the anointing. There is a price to pay for success, and not everybody will be willing to pay that price. There is a consecration that is unique to you, and there are certain things God will not allow you to do. I told you earlier about when I rejected the offering from my mentor, and you might have thought there was nothing wrong in accepting the offering. My mentor even told me later that it was his way of trying to support my ministry.

Through my commitment to the Lord, I knew that my access to his life was already enough support. It was a sign of a covenant I had with God. Not everybody is going to cross that bridge with you. Money is too big for other people to forsake. I say to people, "your NO can be anointed." Your maturity is not seen from the things you say YES to; the stuff you say NO to demonstrate your maturity.

Deprivation is precisely what fasting is about. Certain things are legitimate and reasonable, but God will cause you to deny yourself of them. For example, God would say to Samson, don't cut your hair. Is there anything wrong with cutting your hair? Of course not. It is just a special consecration he had with God. So, Gethsemane is where God will separate from you those who can't bear the consecration, demand, sacrifice, or crushing necessary for where He is taking you to.

At Gethsemane, your mentees will drop off by themselves, and you might be the one that has to say, *'Sit here, wait for me here. I will go alone and come back to meet you.'* You can't carry everybody to where you are going. Some people can't be with you while you are going through your crushing because they will judge you, misunderstand you, and discourage you. All of that can pull you down. So, you have to say, like Jesus,

'Abide here'. He told His disciples to wait for him until He returned.

There is a level of mentorship where people will cross the barriers with you and go where other people cannot go with you. Not everyone will bear the crushing at Gethsemane with you, and some will watch from afar. Recognise that it's okay because they may not understand it now.

Look at the rich man in the Bible that came to Jesus and said he wanted to follow Him. Jesus said he should go home and sell all his property first and give to the poor. If you study scriptures, you will notice that for every other person that came to follow Jesus, Jesus sent them back, but in this case, He asked him to come. The man who was delivered from the demonic possession by legions wanted to follow Jesus, but Jesus asked him to go back and tell his people about the good things God had done for him. So many people tried to join themselves with Jesus, but Jesus sent them back. In other words, Jesus was saying, *'You're not chosen to follow me in this mission at this particular time.'* It takes a level of consecration to follow and be a part of His team.

The point is some people will not be available for the level of your consecration. The anointing upon your life has demanded that dedication, and you are the one that has to say, 'Wait here.' Later, you will realise that when it begins to yield fruit, those same people will say, 'Now I understand'.

5. Those that you will take with you

All the disciples may be with you, but there are people you will have to take further. In verse 37, the Bible says He took Peter, James, and John to go further. He was a mentor to all of them but at different levels of mentorship.

6. Those who can handle your brokenness

The Bible says in verse 38 that he took Peter, James, and John, and He began to be sorrowful. He saw what was ahead and began to experience deep sorrow, and they could share in his distress. Those He left behind at Gethsemane had never seen Him in that condition before and may never have the privilege to see it again.

Not everybody can handle your sorrow. Some people can bear it when you are in deep sorrow, and some can't take it. Some people can't see you in your humanity and still look up to you. Many pastors' kids became bitter toward their parents' ministry because they were exposed to their sorrow when they were unprepared for it. You have to be able to discern who you can take to this level of mentorship. It is a privilege, an honour and a depth that few people get to in relationships.

You know there are two ways to preach the gospel: you can preach the gospel despite your flaws, and you can preach a gospel that presents you as flawless. A lot of people pick the latter. When they preach holiness, they preach it as if they were entirely holy. When they preach integrity, they are criticising everybody else and self-magnifying. We should try to preach from a place of humility and agree that God is building us all and moving us from where we are to where we should be.

I remember one of my mentors. This mentor of mine is one of such people who felt he was better than everybody else, and he presented himself and positioned himself that way. Unfortunately, I had also received him as such. I remember one day, I was criticising another minister to him. I said this person did this and that, and thank God I have got you, and you are not like that. He turned to me and said, '*That is not necessarily true. I am human as well.*'

I was shocked, I could now see him in his humanity, and I couldn't handle it. We had built a relationship for so long upon his infallibility. I struggled to retain my reverence for him, but I couldn't. I couldn't handle his sorrow. This encounter was the first time he was bare before me, and I couldn't take it. The closer I got to him, the more I saw, and I couldn't take it. I developed a song I started singing from that day, and I sing it a lot to my wife and mentees. It says, '*I ain't no super saint.*' It means, look, I am a human being too. Please don't put me in a position where you think I am immune to any level of temptation.

At that same time, I had another mentor who, if he got angry, would get furious in front of me. He never presented himself as faultless. The Bible says, '*Confess your faults one to another*' (James 5:16). So, we have faults, and we should be able to communicate them. There is a healing that is found in the declaration. Some people say, '*No! You must be strong and perfect at all times,*' Once you set yourself in that mode, it is a fickle place. It's a very fragile place to be. Once it is broken and that relationship is finished, it would be tough to restore it, and I am speaking from personal experience.

It was not like I was a judgmental person. I had two mentors at that time; one set himself as infallible and the critic of all other men, and the other was humble enough to come just as he was. I saw worse things by far than this other person did, and I never lost my respect for him for one second.

7. Being alone with the Father

Your number one mentor is God, and you must be willing to be alone with God. No matter how many people surround your life, there must be a level where you are ready to strip everyone else off, and it is just you and God. No man or woman can fulfil this level of mentorship that God alone can accomplish for you. It is the most needful of all forms of mentorship, yet we hardly reach for it. Nothing can replace your aloneness with God. There are certain things that only God can understand about you that no man can ever know.

There is a hierarchy in mentorship. The funniest thing is that at level 3, where people can be offended by you, is where people misrepresent themselves in a mentorship relationship. Peter said he could never be offended by Him and all of the other disciples also disagreed with Jesus. It means they all thought they were at level 6, but they were really at level 3. So, it is crucial that you look at your heart and not overestimate yourself.

Is a mentorship permanent?

The honour is permanent, and every mentorship relationship is for a reason and a season. While the role of their mentoring you might not be permanent, the reverence, the love, and the regard should always be enduring. Close every door gently because you will never know when God will bring you back there in the future. God will take you into places where He will gradually draw you out of particular mentorships. Close that door gently. Close that door with honour and regard.

Some mentorships are permanent, and some mentorships are temporary. God alone determines which is what. Always step away with kindness and with honour.

I will give you a personal example. This same mentor that presented himself as infallible was always picking on every other minister. He was happy only when he despised other people. He was always pulling to compare how he was better than every other person. I don't think he knew what he was doing, but he was crushing everyone. I remember telling him once that I wanted to go to Lagos to visit my parents, and he was like, '*What are you visiting them for?*' He didn't want me to relate with even my biological parents, contrary to what the scriptures say.

When I realised how much this man needed to grow in this area, proximity became more difficult without dishonouring him. So, I brought the matter before God, and God gave me the release to withdraw myself away from that particular relationship. I didn't want to be in a situation where I would be forced to react in dishonour or anger. It was like Samuel and Saul. When your heart is right before God, you will keep on praying for Saul until a time God will tell you, because of your honour, '*Stop weeping for Saul; go and do what I have told you to do.*'

I am not anybody's judge. Sometimes, people can change as time unfolds. God permitted me to withdraw from that relationship, and I had to depart. I departed with honour, and I still reach out to help occasionally, but I do it in a way that will not open the door of intimacy with him. I realised later that it was the same way he would speak about me to others to prop himself up. I went to God in prayer that I didn't want to dishonour that man, and God said I could move on and detach. It hurt me to disconnect.

In other relationships, we just simply drifted apart. This one I just mentioned was deliberate. There were other people I was close to, and God by Himself drew us apart. But then I have had mentorships that have gone to level 6, that have stayed constant in my life for 20 years and 30 years.

How Do We Correct a Wrong Mentoring Relationship?

Sometimes, separation is necessary. Mentoring is like marriage. A marriage can be pushed to the corner in such a way that a temporary break is needed to let things cool down, emotions simmer, and the clouds settle. Then you can start picking the pieces and find out where things went wrong so that you can amend them. I don't ever preach divorce, but I think God can accept some form of separation for a while to facilitate reconciliation. That also applies to mentorship relationships.

There are other mentorship relationships where things going wrong are a sign for you to move elsewhere. But please don't feel you have outgrown somebody like a piece of cloth. Many people think mentors are ATMs, so they perceive the relationship as useless when they have attained more financial success than their mentors. That is so pathetic and shallow. Please, we should always have a humble heart.

Every king needs a prophet, whether in the old testament or the new testament, even as the king and priest God has made you. Prophets never enjoyed the control of affairs as kings did. If you look into the Old Testament, you will see a Nathan being able to rebuke David, a Samuel being able to speak to Saul, etc. The kings could imprison the prophets, and the kings were far more affluent than the prophets, yet the prophets could guide them. These carnal things we look at are just so wrong.

I often give an example of Pa Elton, a Scottish missionary who lived about sixty years in Osun State, Nigeria. He was a spiritual mentor to Pastor E.A. Adeboye, Bishop David Oyedepo, Archbishop Benson Idahosa, the C.U. movement, and many other movements in Nigeria. These people considered this man their mentor. If we regard these carnal considerations, how could someone who has one thousand churches and drives a Rolls Royce ever think about somebody with a Peugeot 404, lives in Osun, and doesn't know how to use email as their mentor?

This is because mentorship is beyond that. It would be best if you never competed with your mentor. I shut down any mentee around me who gives the impression that we are competing. The truth is any sincere mentor should want to make you better than himself. That is the goal in the first place. So, when you start looking down on your mentor, that is a no-no for me. It should be a big NO in mentorship relationships.

What is the level of Vulnerability/Intimacy Between a Mentee and a Mentor

The level of intimacy between a mentor and a mentee is dependent on the level of mentorship that I explained earlier. For instance, some people are there only to eat your fruits. When I discover those kinds of people, I give them my materials (tapes and books) instead of spending time with them. You will not see real mentorship here. The mentorship was never designed to be a burden to crush the mentor. It is supposed to be a relationship of mutual benefit to both parties. Your growth should inspire your mentor. You should be inspired by the wisdom and spiritual input from your mentor, none at the expense of the other.

Take charge of the level of intimacy. It was not the disciples who volunteered that they would stay behind. Jesus had to tell all, except three, of the twelve to '*Stay here till I return.*' It would be best if you were discerning. The Bible says, '*A man without control over his spirit is like a city without walls* (Proverbs 25:28). A city without walls means that anybody can go out and anybody can come in. You have to be proactive with intimacy and preemptive about your vulnerability. I am not saying be very tough. All of us should be aiming to be level 6 mentors and mentees. If nobody can break beyond level 3 with you as a mentor, you have a problem, but you have to know that you don't carry everybody there. Don't just open your life without a measure of proactive control and yielding to God about it. The Bible said that Jesus knew what was in their hearts. You should be like that with your disciples or mentees. Jesus was with Judas at Gethsemane, but he didn't go further. He was one of those Jesus left behind. Be proactive.

How to Improve the Level of Mentorship With Your Mentor

It's not so much what you do but what you are. We are always thinking of what we can do to maintain a relationship when we should be thinking of what we are first. Every time someone asked Jesus, '*What must I do to be saved?*' His reply was always, '*Be born again*'. They were looking for what to do, and He was telling them what to be. We are not human doers; we are human beings. It is much more about what we are than what we do. Concentrate on who you are and what you are, and continually grow.

- Be Humble

- Be Sincere

- Always Reciprocate Value.

In whatever way we can, we must always try to reciprocate value. After that woman fed him and gave him a room in her home, Elisha couldn't rest or sleep unless he blessed her. He asked, 'What can I do for this woman'?

Anyone sincere should always lookout for a way to reward value. Always choose the high road with the people looking up to you or the people you look up to. When you do that, it brings longevity to relationships.

What do you do if your mentor does not believe in a vision you are pursuing?

I must first of all state that you must be submissive and humble enough to receive mentorship. It is best to be easily persuaded by your mentors. Mentors must feel comfortable instructing and correcting those they guide. A stubborn mentee is a double loser who loses the time spent with the mentor and then bears the repercussions of being stubborn.

However, sometimes a mentor's opinion may contradict God's plan or instructions. This situation is not uncommon. That is why I said you should have different mentors. I have mentors that are marriage mentors to us.

A couple who are Christian missionaries from the U.S. who served in Ghana for some years and later moved to Nigeria mentored us in our marriage. They are missionaries, and they evaluate ministry from the perspective of missions that were prevalent in their time. I visit them to help them once every year.

Missions mean so much to them, but they only see missions as Americans going to Africa. They don't see Africans going to America as missions; they regard it as economic expediency. So, it was challenging for me to persuade them otherwise. I loved how they function as a team, and I could learn for my marriage by watching them.

By watching them, I have learned to pick my struggles, that it is not everything I must correct, and I must not be baited into every fight. Some things don't instigate me anymore in my relationship, and I learned this through them. I love how they overlook stuff between each other. I love how they complement each other. They are fantastic marriage mentors and mentors in keeping me humble and real. No matter how high in the clouds your head is, your feet must be touching the ground.

God put so many things in my heart to do that they simply couldn't understand. I had to go to God to know if He indeed asked me to do those things, and I did that sincerely. I didn't disregard their opinion with arrogance. I tried hard to explain that Africa could also reciprocate and return the Gospel to a post-Christian Europe, but they couldn't appreciate that. We didn't share the same view on the matter of missions, and yet I still went ahead and did it.

I don't believe mentorship should be a remote control. I have never done that with anybody, and I am most uncomfortable when someone tries to do that with me. I don't believe anybody is called to create clones of themselves.

There was a man I respected greatly. He was famous and affluent, and God gave me unprecedented access to him. He opened his heart to me and wanted to mentor me, but I had to pull back from being mentored by him because he had one philosophy that would have defined our relationship. Using a verse that stated that a servant could never be greater than his master, he taught that the mentor was always right and that mentors must always be more successful than their mentees, and you can never attain your mentor's level. I knew I could never relate to that.

The truth is we have only one master, which is Jesus Christ. Christ is constantly trying to bring us to His level, not keep us away from attaining His level. The Bible says, '*A son will be greater than his father*'.

There is a measure of sonship that should be part of mentorship where you are constantly looking to see who to build up. I still love and honour him, but I choose to benefit from afar. It just can't go further than that. I had to keep it that way because of what I saw.

So, if somebody believes mentorship is remote control and gets angry with you if you don't do it exactly the way they did, that has gotten into controlling dimensions, and I wouldn't advise that.

The exception to what I just described above is when you are an employee working for someone else. It would be best if you are working for someone else, don't insist on doing it your way. That is unacceptable. But if you are independent and have a mentor, you won't always agree on everything. Similarly, you can't be a church member and insist on developing your private spiritual agenda for the church. There is always order in the things of the Spirit and leadership.

HOW TO ATTRACT THE RIGHT MENTORS IN YOUR LIFE

Dr Samuel Ekundayo

8

Mentorship Must Be Gotten Right

If I have seen further, it is by standing on the shoulders of giants – Isaac Newton

One of the key attributes of this quote is that we need people in our lives who will help us see and go farther than we would be able to go alone. We need mentors in our lives that are capable of helping us rise – rise above our own egos, above our mistakes and errors, above people's approval and rejection combined, above every day challenges that often put us down. I believe one of the ways to rise very quickly in life is to have the right mentors.

I'll be honest to say that I have gotten some mentorship relationships wrong in my life. There were times I rushed into mentorship with someone, and I later realised that they were not right for me. There were no defined values, no alignment with the direction I was going in life, and where God was leading me. So, even though we have seen the importance of getting mentorship right in the first part of this book, it is equally important for you to know how to attract the right mentors into your life.

The right mentors are not necessarily the ones that have a large following (for instance, a million followers on Social Media) or people who are popular. It is important that you get this. The right mentors are simply people that are ahead of you on the journey that God has placed you on. I have followed people who had a large following in times past and I realised that they were not just the right mentors for me. A mentor is not determined by the number of following, but by their ability to lead you right on the path of your purpose. The right mentors for you may not be riding the latest cars or living in mansions but they have the right skills, experience, expertise, and influence to help you in the direction of your purpose. The truth is that they may even be younger than you.

I am an African and age can be a very big deal to us. We often calculate people's influence by their age. This, however, can be very misleading. It was John Maxwell who said that, 'The best mentor for you is someone at your next level'. Mentors are people who are already on the next rung of the ladder that you are climbing.

Therefore, when it comes to attracting the right mentors or influencers into your life, popularity, age or affluence should never be the parameter with which you judge. Don't get me wrong, the right mentors for you may be popular and affluent; there is nothing wrong about that. But, you must not make that the parameter you use in determining if a mentor is right for you or not.

In the next few chapters, I will be shedding light on the principles that will help you attract the right mentors or influencers into your life, no matter the niche you are in or the calling of God on your life. I want you to come along with me.

9

You Must Be A Person Of Value

To attract the right mentors into your life, you must be a person of value. What do I mean by this? At creation, God made every one of us people of value. However, activating that value is not automatic. A person of value is someone who is doing something productive with their lives. The very first mandate God gave to man was to be fruitful. To be fruitful means, to be radically productive. So, if a man is not fruitful, he cannot be valuable. In other words, a person of value is the one that has discovered himself and his gifts. He or She is a person that constantly shows up to add value to lives with their gifts and calling. A person of value is someone who others want to associate with. Nobody wants to relate with someone who is mediocre. If you are not productive with your life, you will very well struggle to attract the right mentors into your life. No matter your potential, what you are doing right now to activate your potential is the attraction for the right mentor into your life.

Let me share a story of how I met a very good friend of mine who is a great man and powerful influence on my life. When I started following him on Instagram, I was always glued to what he was saying and doing. I must have turned on my post notification to make sure I did not miss any of his posts. Out of the blue, one day, I realized he followed me back. I was blown away. I never saw it coming. After a while, I had to ask him why he followed me back, because as at the time he followed me, I only had just about a thousand-plus followers. So, I was really curious. He said to me, '*Dr. Sam, I have been watching you for a whole year now and I kept asking myself if this guy was genuine and consistent with his message or one of those people that just comes and goes and we never hear of them again'*

As a person of value, it means you are shinning your light, you are fulfilling purpose, and you are consistent and committed to your calling and message. This is something you do not do to attract people, but to give expression to your purpose. You are enjoying yourself while at it; feeling fulfilled, and inspired to do more every day. You are busy focused on your calling, whether people are paying attention or not. I say this because you need to know that if you are doing it to attract people, you will soon get discouraged when the people you are trying to attract refuse to look your way or fail to engage with what you're doing. The funny thing is that some of the people you are trying to attract, who may not be forthcoming yet, peradventure are checking to see with curiousity if you are genuine. They are curious to see if you are serious and committed to your purpose. The truth is, no one likes to be associated to a lazy or mediocre mind.

In fact, I realised that Jesus never called a lazy person to himself. All of the disciples of Jesus were people who were busy professionals in their fields. He saw Peter and Andrew fishing. They were busy. He called them to follow Him so He could turn what they were already doing into something of greater and eternal value. While they were trained to catch fishes, He turned them to fishers of men such that they are still affecting generations beyond them thousands of years after.

If you want to attract the right mentors into your life, you cannot afford not to be committed and consistent with your purpose. If you only show up for a while then disappear into thin air later, you will never be able to attract the right mentors into your life. To the glory of God, a lot of people reach out to me on almost a daily basis to mentor them; I receive messages in my DM on Facebook, Instagram and LinkedIn. The first thing I do when I get such messages is to go through the profiles of those people on social media.

Do they look like they have discovered their purpose? Do they look like they know their identity? Are they committed to and consistent with their messages? Do they look like they know what they are doing with their lives? These are the questions I ask myself as I go through their profiles. Let me quickly state here, especially for young people, that you must take your social media handles seriously. They are your platforms and you must utilize them well. They represent you and give the world an impression of you. Don't let anyone tag you anyhow on things that do not align with your core values or the calling of God on your life. If they do, decline and delete such tags. Imagine that you have a store where you sell things, I am sure you would want to make it clean and attractive to your customers. That is the same way you should treat your social media platforms and timelines. Let people come and all they see is that you are full of value. This is how potential mentors will be attracted to you.

Remember the story of the influencer who is now my friend that I mentioned earlier. He studied me for 12 months just to see if I was genuine. When he had ascertained that, he reached out to connect with me. Our friendship started growing, and now we do things together. To attract people of value into your life, you must be a person of value too. The way things work on social media these days, people you send a friend request to or start following will often search you out. They want to know if you are a person of value before they accept your request to connect or follow you back. I believe they are not trying to be condescending or judgmental, they are instead being deliberate about their association. Like Jim Rohn said, '*You are the average of the five people you spend the most time with*'

One of my mentors who had been watching the episodes of *Motivitality* (My short video teachings on social media), stumbled on an episode that really inspired him one day. He didn't only like the post, he actually commented thus, 'This truly blessed me'. I was blown away, because I am talking about someone way older than me and more accomplished. It felt good to have someone who I looked up to getting blessed by my message. What I did was to reach out to the person in his DM on Instagram to appreciate him for his comment on my video. I didn't take that gesture for granted. The right thing to do is to interact with people of value who show interest in what you are doing. Reach out to them and appreciate them. Their feedback to you shows that they have recognised you as a person of value and you need to be consistent if you are going to continue to attract people like them.

10

Invest In Their Materials

Sometimes, there are people you are clearly after because you want them to mentor you. You know the value they carry and you know that you need that value in your life especially in terms of where God is taking you. They carry what you desire and you will cherish them being your mentor. For these kind of people, find a way to invest in their materials; add value to what they are doing. I love the words of Fela Durotoye, 'When you pay for what people are doing, you are connecting to what they are doing, but when you sow directly into their lives, you are connecting to their roots'. To connect to the root of something or someone means to dig deep. This will cost you something. Investing into the people you desire to mentor you is like touching them the way that woman with the issue of blood touched Jesus. You need to touch them differently.

Let me take you into that story real quick. Jesus was in a very crowded place, on his way to heal someone else's daughter. See, Jesus was not even reaching out to the woman or had any intention of healing her. He was focused on somewhere and something else, when the woman said to herself, "I am not going to let this opportunity pass me by. I have to reach out and touch Him with everything I've got". All she could get was the helm of Jesus' garment and that was enough, in fact more than enough for her. She touched Jesus differently. I mean, within a large crowd, everything was touching and pressing in on Jesus but only one touch carried weight and stopped Him in His tracks! He had to ask, "who touched me!" The rest, as they say, is history.

Just like that story, the mentor you are after may not be looking for you or have any intention of meeting or connecting with you. They may be going about their own business, busy and focused but you can touch them differently. You can be that person that would stop them in their tracks enough to get their attention. While everyone else is in their DMs saying, 'Hello, sir', 'Hi, sir', etc., you should be asking, how can I touch them differently such that they will feel my touch amidst many other touches? Jesus felt that woman's touch even though there were a lot of people touching him.

Let me say that I am not referring to you being desperate. You won't attract the right mentors into your life by desperation. Touch your mentors uniquely through investing in them and their products, not by desperation. Invest into their books, programmes, courses, etc. How can you desire someone to be your mentor and you have refused to read the books they have written (including the free ones), attend the programmes they organise, sign up for their courses, etc.? The way you show that you truly value them is to invest in the value they are offering. This also arms you with the necessary information about them so that the day you finally get the opportunity reach out to or meet them, you are asking the right questions and saying the right things. You are able to easily connect with them because you are speaking their language based on what you already know about them.

Some investments in life are worth making if you are going to connect with the right people in your life. Do not be the type of person who spends a lot of money on things that do not matter and call the things that matter expensive. If you want to connect with a potential mentor, you must seem their materials a worthy investment for your journey in life. I have and still purchase some courses because I desire to connect with the trainer or coach. I realise this gesture of investing in their materials gets me close to them quicker than I could have if I didn't. Just like the analogy of the woman with the issue of blood, investing in their materials helped me to touch them differently.

The truth is, most people in life are looking for free and cheap things. They only want to do what won't bother them or cause them to go out of their way. If you really see that potential mentor as the ladder to that next stage of your calling, you must be willing to go out of your way, you must be willing to invest. Find out what they have on sale at the moment, find out what books they've written, and invest in them; it would help you to connect faster and more genuinely. It shows you are committed to the process of having them as your mentor, and without their consent to mentoring you, you are ready to kickstart the processing by availing yourself of the resources they have available. That says a lot about who you are.

11

Meet A Dire Need

The deepest of human connections is often based on mutual fulfilment of needs. If you are meeting a need in someone's life, you are always going to be valuable to them. On that note, it is crucial to know that everyone on the surface on the earth has a need. No matter how high and mighty they are, every man has a need. Even God has a need. That is why He always seeks for a man, "Whom shall I send, and who will go for us?" One way to tap into the favour of God is to meet His needs through service. So, to connect deeply with anyone, find out what need they have that you can meet, and you will become increasingly valuable to them. Jesus' mandate on earth required disciples who would take the gospel from Him and spread it to the whole earth after He went back to heaven. At the same time, man was desperately in need of a saviour, and Jesus was the answer to that need. The connection of Jesus to His disciples was on the platform of this fulfilment of needs.

Some needs are very pressing or urgent. They are dire needs and meeting them brings a greater satisfaction to the person in need and elicits a deep sense of appreciation that makes the person in need connect with the person who met the need. Many times, Jesus needed things to be done like needing a boat, needing a donkey, needing company, etc. and his disciples always rose up to the task. You must learn to meet a dire need.

A dire need is not necessarily monetary. It may just be you volunteering to help out. For instance, the person who you desire as a mentor may be organizing a workshop or conference. Instead of just registering to be a part of the conference or workshop, you can indicate interest to serve in any capacity that can help the success of such meetings. That meeting is your opportunity to get closer to that person.

Send a message ahead. Note that there is the need to introduce yourself the first time you are reaching out to anyone in their DMs. Some of our young people today are very funny or sometimes rude when they reach out to people who are supposed to be their potential mentors. 'Hello, sir', 'Hi, sir', 'Hello, dear', 'Greetings, sir', 'Morning, sir', etc. are not the right ways to initiate a conversation with someone who you desire to mentor you. Why not try something like this:

'Hello, sir. My name is Dr. Samuel Ekundayo. I help people discover their purpose so that they can maximise their potentials. I have been following you for a while now and I have seen that you have the ingredients that can help me on my journey in life. Please, I would like to know if there is any way I can be of service to you. Thank you'

Don't go with your need first. Have a service-first mentality where what is genuinely on your mind is how you can be of help to this person you desire as a mentor.

Adding value and *serving* are two uncommon words that are sweet to the hearing of anyone. These are words that people hardly use today, but will attract anyone to you.

Once again, let me reiterate that if you follow someone close enough through reading their books, listening to their teachings, watching their videos, following their lives, and so on, you will discover their needs. And you will always get the attention of the person whose needs you meet. It is a natural phenomenon.

Let me share a story of another mentor of mine. At the time of this incident, he had not yet agreed to mentor me. So, I went to visit him one day and he took me to his office. Then, I realised that there was this particular thing he had been wanting to do for weeks which had been a struggle for him. As God would have it, that area of need was where I was very good at. All I did was to tell him that I could help him. I volunteered to help. What he had been struggling with for weeks was resolved in about one hour. He was so excited that he said, 'Samuel, I feel like keeping you in my house'. The rest is history. Today, he is one of the most influential persons in my life.

Another mentor of mine had a vision for his birthday to mentor hundreds of people, and he needed someone to help lead the initiative. Interestingly, I was not the first choice but the person chosen could not do it for reasons beyond her control so the baton was passed to me. I took it with joy and excitement, not because I didn't have anything to do but because I knew it would present me the opportunity to be close to my mentor. I gave it my best, and you guessed right, it helped me connect deeper with him. In fact, through leading that initiative for him, I learned so much than I would have learned just watching others do it. Some of those lessons I am now applying in my own visions and expressions.

Anytime you sense or hear about a need of a potential mentor, do not hide your face. So many people run away from service not knowing they are running away from their own next level. So many people have denied themselves their next level because they dodge whenever the question is asked, "whom shall I send". I love Isaiah's response in the bible, and that should be your response too. With excitement and passion, he said, "I, Here am I; send me". You must have the attitude of willingness whenever you see a need that needs to be met. It is an uncommon attitude that will raise your altitude in life.

There are some young people who are now my mentees because of this attitude. For instance, one of my mentees who is a gifted graphics designer connected with me like every business person would. He was introduced to me because he rendered a paid service. He designed a book cover for a manuscript I had just completed at the time. Upon completing the cover, even though I paid him, several months later when I organized a conference, he made himself available at no charge. He saw it as an opportunity to meet a need, and he literally gave his heart to the work. I was very impressed; like the woman with the issue of blood, he touched me differently. Today, both of us are very close; and I can say with joy, he is a mentee in whom I'm well pleased. To the glory of God, both of our lives have been better for it.

12

Give A Gift

This is different from serving or meeting a dire need. You need to learn to give a gift to the person you desire to mentor you. This reminds me of the story of the woman who lavished an expensive oil on Jesus' feet in the presence of people. She didn't mind what people thought about her. She was unashamed about it. She even wiped the oil with her hair. The act was so precious to Jesus that He promised that wherever the gospel goes, her name will also be mentioned. A mentor willingly gives you his name (through endorsements or writing forewords), by recommending you to others, etc.

The Bible succinctly put it that 'The gift of a man makes room for him and brings him before great men'

(Proverbs 18:16). Stinginess won't get you anywhere. While I was still growing up in our home, my dad would give us money in envelopes to give to any minister that came to minister in our church. It became a family culture. Of recent, one of those ministers was asking me if I knew why he would never forget my family. "I didn't know why, sir", I answered. Then, he took me down memory lane, reminding me how he came to minister in our church then and we (my siblings and I) brought envelopes to him on our knees. This was something I had completely forgotten. That singular act didn't leave this minister and as a result, he started counselling and mentoring me. The gesture meant a lot to him, even though I had completely forgotten about it. I couldn't even remember how old I was then, maybe 12 or 14. The money wasn't even mine, it was my parents'. The gift of a man indeed makes room for him.

Some people today are quick to say, 'I don't have enough' or 'I can't afford it'. They can't just bring themselves to invest in what matters. They are not willing to stretch or sacrifice to commit their money or resources to a cause like gifting people things. It is not easy, I know but who says it has to be easy? Great things will cost you and you have to learn this. You don't need to wait until you have much before you give or invest. You start giving from the little that you have. That is the way to have more. He who is faithful in little will be faithful in much.

David said he won't give to God what will not cost him something. If your gift does not cost you something, then it is not a gift. There is another mentor of mine in New Zealand who I met while I was still a student. I couldn't afford much then. So, there was this particular season when all I had was 100 dollars and I got this nudge in my spirit to give him 50 dollars. I knew it was God leading me to do so. Let me quickly state here that the devil can never lead you to give to people. It is against the devil's nature to give without expecting anything in return. His specialty is to steal from people. His purpose is expressly stated in John 10:10 – "The thief comes only to steal and kill and destroy". So, when you have a prompting to give something to someone, don't think it is the devil. It is God, especially when it's motivated by love and not the desire to get something back in return.

What I didn't realise when I gave that money, even though it was not easy for me considering what I had left and how much I was earning as a student, was that the man and his family didn't have what they were going to eat after church that day. It was four years later that this man reminded me of that gesture which I had completely forgotten about. He reiterated that it was that money that helped them eat that day and it meant a lot to him. You can imagine that even though it was hard for me to give that money, I had completely forgotten about it. The giver may forget, but the receiver of such timely, life-saving gifts don't forget. My mentor now has multiple houses in New Zealand

and is living well with his family. We are now very close like a family.

One of the ways to attract the right mentors into your life is by giving gifts. Don't miss the opportunity to give. Giving could mean you're meeting a need without you even knowing it. Give without expecting anything in return and watch how your gift would pave way for you, if not now, in the future. The word of God is truth, and it never lies, so if it says, your gift will make room for you, it surely will; it may not be now, but in time, it will.

13

Be Visible - Follow Genuinely

Be visible, but don't be desperate. I know people who are desperate. Whatever you do for that potential mentor, do it genuinely. If you want to share their posts, do so sincerely, not even because you want them to mentor you; share them because they bless you and you would like to inspire others with them. Do it as a potential protégé who is truly taking in what they are teaching. I have come to realise that whatever does not come out of desperation eventually works. The reason is because since it's not forced, you are able to maintain that attitude and character even when they don't seem to notice or accept to mentor you.

For instance, if that potential mentor is doing a live video on social media, ensure that you watch it, even if it is the replay that you're able to catch. If they are running a course, try to sign up for it. Be in their faces in a positive way, and not desperately. Following them closely is a sign that you truly value them (their message or ministry). There are certain people's videos I share, because I truly value them, but I also understand that it will get the attention of my potential mentor, because they are human and can be touched by such gestures.

There is a warning here. You must never feel entitled because of what you do for them. Don't expect that because you have been sharing their posts then they should automatically have your time, accept to mentor you, or give you money in return. They reserve the right to do whatever they want to do. You are the one seeking to be mentored, not the other way round. So, whatever you do, do it without expecting anything in return. Keep doing what you do for them sincerely and out of a good heart, and one day you may receive their call or message.

Be intentional about learning from them. Peter replied Jesus, when He asked if they were not going to leave too (like some others who had promised to follow Jesus left) as a result of his hard teaching, that only He had the word of life. By following them, engaging their posts, sharing their posts, etc. you are showing them that they have what you need and you are following them to grasp that thing.

Elisha demonstrated this when he followed Elijah passionately. Even though he was not guaranteed to get what he wanted from Elijah, he never stopped following. He shunned every distraction and was an wholehearted follower, even when the sons of the prophets were trying to discourage him.

14

Pray For Them Intentionally

This is a principle. Anyone that you are intentionally praying for, your spirit will attract or connect to their spirit. This is because prayer is a spiritual exercise. It is spirit communicating with spirit. For instance, if you want to connect with me and you start praying for me, my family, my ministry, etc. genuinely, our spirits will finally touch or connect.

There's a record in scripture about Job that says, "When Job prayed for his friends, the LORD restored his fortunes. In fact, the LORD gave him twice as much as before!" [Job 42:10]. I believe God allowed this to be recorded intentionally for us. When you pray for people, there is a resultant effect that is advantageous to you. Job started to pray for his friends, and things turn around for him. I believe if you are intentional in praying for that potential mentor – praying for their ministry, family, careers, health and so on – you will not just experience a turnaround in your life but your spirit will connect to theirs. Our spirit bears witness that we're children of God, so when people of the same spirit connect spiritually, great things happen.

There was a time in my life that I was intentioanlly praying for a mentor of mine (who wasn't mentoring me yet at the time) regularly. There came a time I was in a dire need. I needed transport to go somewhere urgent and I didn't have the money. I called my parents back home in Nigeria and I was crying because I was frustrated. My parents suggested that I should call that mentor. I obeyed and called him and as God would have it that day, he had just driven past where I was, so he turned back to pick me and took me where I was going. From that day onward, something changed in our relationship and I would like to think it was because I had been praying for him and that day was just the full connection beyond our spirits into the physical realm. Today, I am a son to him, and he, a father to me. This all started by praying for him and his family and I still do. Prayer is an investment. So, you can invest prayer into your potential mentor and you will see the returns soon.

As believers, one of the powers God has given to us that we often take for granted is the power of prayer, which gives us access to the spirit realm. It works because the spirit realm controls the physical. A major component of our dominion as children of God is our place in prayer. If you want to see anything physically manifest, be intentional about praying about it. Remember the Bible says, "The king's heart is in the hand of the Lord, as the rivers of water: he turneth it whithersoever he will." [Proverbs 21:1]. God has the heart of every man in His hands. So, if you want to connect to any man, you might as well talk to the God who has their hearts in His hand first. God can make people fall in love with you, and they won't even be able to explain why.

I am reminded of the time the Isrealites were going to leave Egypt, and God told Moses to tell them to demand anything they wanted from the Egyptians. They demanded precious things like gold, silver, etc., and they were given to the point the bible recorded that at the time of their leaving, they had impoverished the Egyptians. In other words, the Egyptians gave without thinking because God had control of their hearts to give everything the Israelites had demanded of them. This again goes to prove, if you consult in prayer with the God who holds the hearts of all men in His hand, you could secure the heart of that potential mentor. It's a price to pay, and if you can pay it, God may just honour your sacrifice.

15

Be Committed To Learning

Nobody wants to mentor someone who is not learning or growing. How can you desire mentoring without been committed to learning? It just doesn't add up – I mean, the very reason to be mentored is for you to grow and maximise your potential. So, if you are not already taking responsibility for your gowth, then, you do not deserve to be mentored.

I remember someone who reached out to me recently and said, 'Dr. Sam, I am not a book person' How on earth will you not be a reader if you really desire to grow and become a leader? To be successful in life, you must read. You must be committed to learning. It is actually your commitment to continuous learning that will put you in the face of a potential mentor. It is your commitment that will make you sacrifice to get the money to register for their courses or programs, or motivate you to buy and read their books, etc. This way, when you finally get to meet them, you will have a common ground, and you would have enough to say or ask that will attract them to you.

Recently, I had a phone call with Rev. Sam Adeyemi. It was my mentor, Bishop Alonge, that connected us. That call lasted for about 30 minutes. During that call, Rev. Sam was sharing some deep revelation and to the glory of God, I was able to make contributions that made sense. It was a situation of deep calling unto deep because I had been learning from him for years, since I was in High School. I had read his books. I was able to ask him relatable questions because I was learned, not just generally but from his wealth of knowledge.

Paul, who was a mentor to Timothy, instructed Timothy to study to show himself approved (2 Timothy 2:15) There is a level of study you must do for you to be approved. Whatever you do, you commit to studying what is required of you. You must be well grounded in your niche so much that when you finally get the chance to meet that one person that matters in your field and can serve as your mentor, you will have something meaningful to say; something that can command attention. I will not accept to mentor a mediocre or someone who is not committed to their growth because I am not lazy in learning myself.

To the glory of God, I have read close to 50 books on purpose and I am still reading. I still search and shop for books on purpose. I just want to read every material I can find on purpose no matter who the author is, because I want to know everything there is to know about the subject. I am studying to show myself approved.

There was a time I was preaching a message on Instagram Live and Pastor Wole Oladiyun – the general overseer of CLAM (Christ Living spring Apostolic Ministry), one of the fastest Pentecostal churches in Nigeria – was watching. Let me quickly say here that whatever you do as a person of value, give your whole attention to it, pour all your energy and knowledge into it, because you don't know who will be watching or listening while you are at it. That day, Pastor Wole Oladiyun was watching and I didn't know. At a point, he started commenting and one of the things he typed was, 'Who is this young man? He is anointed'! 'Get me this young man. The world needs to hear him' I was shocked when I realised this.

The only way this can happen is if you are a person of depth. Deep calls unto deep. When a deep person encounters another deep person, there is always a connection. This reminds me of the story in the Bible [Luke 1:41] when the baby in Elizabeth leaped at the sound of Mary's (the mother of Jesus) greeting; a sign that the two babies connected while they were still in the womb. There are people you meet and the seed of what you're carrying would leap because of the seed inside of them but this is brought about by the depth of the conversation. What triggered the leaping of the babies was the greetings exchanged by their mothers.

Some people never study or read and they expect success to jump on them. That's not possible. There are people who God has revealed their message to the world to, but are not reading about it. They are not studying. They are not listening to anyone who is ahead in that field. They don't have mentors in their field. Oh, I love how John Maxwell puts it; he said, 'Never mentor anyone who doesn't know where they are going. It is a dead end'. One major sign that a person does not know where he or she is headed is when they are not committed to growth and learning. Nobody wants to mentor a dead end. A dead end is the end of a road or passage from which no exit is possible. In other words, it is a road that leads nowhere. Don't be a dead end! Commit to growth and learning, and you will attract the right mentors.

You cannot be a leader and not be a reader. If you don't know how to read, learn how to. One person that is adept in this area is Jim Kwik. He has a lot of videos on You Tube that can help you learn about reading and memory. I learned how to read fast from him, and it changed my life.

Know How To Ask The Right Questions

Questions open doors. If you ask the right questions, you will get the right answers. I have different mentors for different areas of my life. Once in a while I would have questions written down to ask my mentors. Whenever I get the opportunity, I would request for a time with them to ask my questions. At such times, I am always prepared to listen to their wisdom and guidance. Let me state that your mentors may not have the answers to all of your questions, but the insights they will give you could make all the difference. These insights could help you connect the dots that would eventually lead you to the answer.

You must learn how to ask intelligent questions and you must prepare your questions in advance. Don't ever meet your mentors without a question you are prepared to ask. One of the ways to make a mentor-mentee relationship blossom is for the mentee to ask intelligent questions. It shows that you are willing to learn, willing to sit at their feet.

The disciples of Jesus demonstrated this a lot. Often, when Jesus had taught in parables to the crowd, they would go back to Him to ask for clarifications. They would often do this when the crowds had left Jesus and they're alone with Him. My favorite of such moments was recorded in Matthew 13. In verse 10, the disciples went to Jesus and asked Him why He often told stories when he spoke to the crowd. Jesus did not condemn them for asking such a question. Instead, He shared with them a mystery that further buttressed the importance of mentorship. Jesus said, the crowds have their hearts hardened and so cannot understand the mysteries of the Kingdom of Heaven; as only His disciples were permitted to understand. The disciples had paid the price to understand such mysteries because they had left everything to follow Him, unlike the crowds who were only there to get whatever they could glean from Jesus and return back to their vomits.

Jesus' words are worth studying; speaking about the crowd, He said, "for they look, but they don't really see. They hear but they don't really listen or understand. True mentees are ready to see beyond what is being illustrated, to listen and not just hear, and to comprehend matters of the heart however mysterious they come across. It could also be seen in their hunger to understand by asking germane and intelligent questions.

I have come to understand that people who ask the right questions are often people who have developed the art of listening. Listening is indeed an art; it requires being conscious, present and mindful. A true mentee must develop this art. It's not enough to just ask questions but you must listen for the mysteries in your mentors words in order to ask the right questions. Curious like a child, you must be genuine in your desire to understand all that is being passed on.

We saw this childlike desire in the manner in which Mary chose to sit at the feet of Jesus when He came visiting them. You see, Mary and Martha were sisters, very good friends of Jesus. Jesus came visiting and Martha was very busy, in the words of the scripture, "anxious and trouble about many things" [Luke 10:4]. We saw a different mindset in Mary, who sat quietly at the feet of Jesus, gazing intently with curious desire to glean all that was possible from Him, knowing it was such a rare opportunity of a lifetime. Mary's pose is such that every mentee must have with their mentor – childlike, ready, eager, and intentional about gleaning everything possible. This is the key to listening well enough to ask the right questions that bring out the depth of their wisdom. As the Bible rightly posits, "deep calls unto deep".

I once heard Rev Sam Adeyemi say, "a true mentee listens beyond the words of the mentor". Everyone listens for the word perhaps but when you find yourself listening beyond the words, and almost discerning the intent and heart behind their words, you likely have been following closely enough.

As a mentee, like Jesus' disciples, you need to learn to ask the right questions. You need to learn and practice the art of intentional listening so you can ask the right questions. Also, your questions should be sensible and intelligent. Don't ask your mentors questions that you can probably find on Google. Let your depth call for more from them. This is how you grow in wisdom.

17

Have A Good Attitude

It is important that you approach your mentors with humility and politeness (especially when you are just meeting them for the first time). Even if you are older than the supposed mentor, please be humble and have a good attitude. Nobody will accept to mentor someone with a poor attitude. Barbara Johnson said that, '*Attitude is the minds paintbrush; it can colour any situation*'. Your attitude can be seen in anything you do, and if you don't have a good attitude, you cannot attract good mentors. Your attitude has the power to paint your life bad or good.

I get requests to mentor people from time to time, and I often would decline first time on the account that I do not know them. I have a custom reply, which is,

"I do not know you enough to know if you're humble and teachable to accept to mentor you". That is actually the truth. It takes knowing someone well enough to know how teachable they are. Mentoring someone who is not teachable would be a disaster.

You need to be teachable. You cannot attract the right mentors if you are not teachable. To be teachable means you are very willing to learn. You desire to be taught. Some people just want to do all the speaking when they are with their mentors. They know it all, and would even try to correct their mentors. This is a very poor attitude.

You must get rid of entitlement mentality. You must also remember that no one owes you anything. Yes, the fact that you request to be mentored does not mean the person has to accept. They reserve the right to accept or decline your request. So, you need to have that at the back of your mind and respect the potential mentor's decision in advance.

Someone reached out to me in my DM sometime ago and said, 'Hello, sir. I want you to mentor me'. That was all he said. He didn't introduce himself, or said anything further. I felt, he'd approached me as if it was his right that I accept to mentor him. That's not the right way to approach a potential mentor. That's a wrong attitude to have; the attitude of entitlement. Again, no one owes you their time or their affection. It's a great privilege for you to be mentored, and you must treat the request to be mentored with that in mind.

The fact that you bought someone's book doesn't mean they should give you their time. The fact that you paid for their course does not mean they must mentor you. If you think they are obliged to because you purchased their resources or products, then you are being entitled, and that attitude will not get you far. You are not doing the mentor a favour; they are the ones doing you a favour, and you have to accord them that respect and honour.

One of my core values is honouring people. Those who are close to me know this. I am quite vocal about it to those who work for me, and those I mentor. Should I sense any iota of dishonour from someone, I cut off from them without looking back. If I am going to accept to mentor anyone, I am always eager to see they hold similar value too. Irrespective of whether the honour code is a core value of your potential mentor or not, you must hold this very dear to you. When you honour and value people, you are likely to be honoured and valued in return, and this will get you into some quarters that matter in life. I cannot tell you how many doors honouring people has opened for me. I believe it would open doors for you too, if you adopt it.

Do not be entitled. The attitude or mentality of entitlement will get you no where, and it would make you lose people instead of gaining their approval.

Another very important point before concluding this chapter is, don't be tempted to ask money from your mentor. No matter how desperate you are. It is not a good omen and many people have closed doors on themselves because of this. Some young people are opportunists and don't care who they take advantage of, as long as they get what they want. This kind of attitude won't get you very far in life. Learn to put your needs aside when approaching a potential mentor. They are in your life to guide you not to provide for you. If they willingly offer, then that's not a problem but you should not be asking.

18

Pray for Favour

You may have done the ten things I have mentioned earlier, but you can never take away the place of favour. Concerning Jesus, it was said, "and Jesus increased in wisdom and stature, and in favour with God and man" (Luke 2:52 KJV). You may wonder why Jesus (God in human form) needed favour with men. It's because favour is important as long as you're here in the flesh. In the realms of men, favour is critical to your success.

You need to ask God for the favour of men. Pray that the hearts of potential mentors will be open to you. Anything God would do in your life; He would do through men. Let me say that again, anything you have prayed to or believed God for will most likely be answered through men. I feel like there are sometimes

God has actually answered our prayers but our attitudes with men may have hindered the manifestations of our prayers. So, without the gift of men, we are nothing.

I am reminded of two stories in the Bible that depicted this very well. One was the recommendation David received to gain appointment to work in the palace for King Saul. One of Saul's servants had to recommend David, and his words relayed the favour David got in his sights. He said, "I have seen a son of Jesse of Bethlehem who knows how to play the lyre. He is a brave man and a warrior. He speaks well and is a fine-looking man. And the LORD is with him" [1 Samuel 16:18]. Can you imagine if David had once been rude to that servant of Saul? I am sure he would not have provided such recommendation to the king. The second one was the butler who recommended Joseph to Pharoah. He had encountered Joseph in the prison. Even though it took him two years to remember Joseph, he recalled the experience that got him out of prison, owing to Joseph's benevolence. His kind words to Pharoah about Joseph got him to the palace. Imagine if Joseph had been cruel to him in prison?

I dare say once again, whatever God would do in your life, he would use men. Learn to pray and ask God for favour in the sight of men, just as much as you ask for God's favour. Favour is a critical factor in life. Favour helps us to get things with ease; favour helps us to attract the good sides of people.

And as you have read through the pages of this book, you are going to need God to favour you in the sight of the right mentors for them to accept to mentor you. Your attitude can help you earn their favour. Also, ask God for favour in the place of prayer as favour in the sight of the right mentor can deliver you from years of toiling.

I believe in you.